Twayne's United States Authors Series

Sylvia E. Bowman, *Editor*

INDIANA UNIVERSITY

James A. Michener

JAMES A. MICHENER

by A. GROVE DAY
University of Hawaii

 60

Twayne Publishers, Inc.   ::   New York

813
Day

For

Carl Stroven

Senior Professor of English and Librarian

University of Hawaii

and friend of forty years

Preface

EVERYONE WHO READS or goes to the movies or looks
at television is aware that James A. Michener is one of
the most popular writers of our generation. The reader recalls
that his first book, *Tales of the South Pacific,* was hailed as the
best World War II novel from the Pacific, was awarded the
Pulitzer Prize for fiction, and was made into a smash Broadway
musical play, and also a film. He knows Michener is a world
traveler who has written dozens of articles for magazines, as
well as other books like *The Fires of Spring, Return to Paradise,
The Bridges at Toko-Ri, Sayonara,* and the big novel *Hawaii.*
All his books have been reprinted in paperback editions in
English, and his words have entertained millions around the
world not only in that language but in translations into a dozen
other languages.

Undoubtedly the time has come to examine the body of this
man's work and to evaluate his achievement. Immediate and
wide popularity does not necessarily brand an author as beneath
criticism. Aside from a few reviews in periodicals, no critical
attention has been given to Michener (for instance, only two
brief articles are listed under his name in the annual PMLA
bibliographies). The first special problem tackled in this book,
then, is: How much can be done in making a definitive critical
estimate in a pioneering study? One man's answer, based on my
rereading in chronological order of some two million words by
Michener—as well as on a personal relationship extending over
fifteen years—will be found in the following pages.

A second main question arising from this study is: Can any
useful judgments be made about an author who is still writing
at the top of his bent and who, perhaps, might still publish
his best book? To this I can only reply that I shall gladly revise
any of my opinions when further grounds are offered for
doing so.

A third question arises, the answer to which will be of great
fascination not only to the general reader but to the aspiring
writer and the student of literature. This is: What is the
"secret" of Michener's broad, sustained popularity as an author?

Is it merely good luck, or a gift for the right word, or a sense of timing that enables him to anticipate what millions of readers will enjoy at the time his book is put on the market? Is it, perhaps, the result of a painstaking apprenticeship in the craft of writing and the application of a retentive memory and a fine intellect to the task of reporting the world with skill, versatility, and warmth? Is it—as appears again and again on the following pages—that through all of Michener's work runs a strong theme associated with the biggest question in the world today: How can we best get along with our human brothers of all races and creeds, avoiding prejudice and eradicating stupid bias? Michener has never known who his parents were; and it is quite probable that, unable to solve the mystery of his own origin, he has been more free than most American writers of our generation to put himself in the shoes or sandals of the hundreds of millions of people on earth who are not of Anglo-Saxon Christian ancestry.

Although I have a high opinion of Michener's contribution to our literature, I have here been concerned less with booming Michener shares on some sort of literary stock exchange than with trying to help his many readers to discover his ideas and to appreciate the richness of many other qualities of his works. As a writer and professor myself, I am as involved as anyone with the glaring fact that too many people read but do not comprehend—and that many who comprehend do not appreciate.

One contribution of the present volume, if rather a pedestrian one, is the Bibliography, which is the first to be compiled on Michener with any attempt at completeness. Those who wish to follow my reading trail have here the signposts. Another feature, in addition to my analyses of all the main writings of this author, is the attempt to collect from many places his comments on his art; the result is to be found in the chapter called "How to Be a Writer." Still another unique aspect of this book is that my lengthy friendship with Michener has given me the opportunity to put on record a number of his remarks from personal letters and from conversations taking place in Honolulu, Bucks County, and spots in between. Seldom has a critic been free to obtain such full access to all the materials on his author and, at the same time, been so free to express value judgments on their worth.

A. Grove Day

University of Hawaii

Acknowledgments

Grateful acknowledgment is made to the author and to Random House, Inc., for permission to use throughout this volume quotations from these copyrighted works of James A. Michener: *Selected Writings, The Fires of Spring, Return to Paradise, The Voice of Asia, The Bridges at Toko-Ri, Sayonara, The Floating World, The Bridge at Andau, Rascals in Paradise, Hawaii,* and *Report of the County Chairman.* Special acknowledgment is also made to the author and The Macmillan Company for permission to use quotations from *Tales of the South Pacific,* copyright 1947.

Quotations in Chapter 8 from "The Chances Against the Beginning Writer" from *The Writer's Book,* copyright 1950, are used with the kind permission of the author, The Authors Guild, and Harper & Row. Quotations in the same chapter from an article in *Northwest Review* are used by permission of that journal and Mr. Michener.

Quotations appearing from the columns of *Saturday Evening Post, Holiday, Reader's Digest, Saturday Review,* New York *Times,* New York *Herald-Tribune,* Chicago *Sunday Tribune, Catholic World, New Republic, Newsweek, Christian Science Monitor,* San Francisco *Chronicle,* Honolulu *Star-Bulletin* and Honolulu *Advertiser* are used by permission of the publishers. Mr. Bob Krauss and Mrs. Clarice B. Taylor have kindly consented to permit quotations from articles appearing in *Paradise of the Pacific* (Honolulu). I am most of all indebted to Mr. Michener for blanket permission to quote from any of his printed works or manuscripts.

Acknowledgment is also gratefully made to the Research Committee of the University of Hawaii for recommending the allowance of time to carry on research on the present volume.

Contents

Chronology

1907? James A. Michener born in New York City, February 3?

1921 Hitch-hiked through forty-five states.

1925 Graduated from Doylestown, Pennsylvania, high school.

1929 Bachelor of Arts in English and history, *summa cum laude,* Swarthmore College (Phi Beta Kappa).

1930- Graduate research at University of Pennsylvania, Univer-
1933 sity of Virginia, Ohio State University, Harvard, University of St. Andrew's (Scotland), University of Siena (Italy). Lippincott Traveling Fellowship.

1933- Teacher, George School, Doylestown, Pennsylvania.
1936

1935 Married Patti Koon.

1936 Master of Arts, Colorado State College of Education.

1936- Associate Professor of Education, Colorado State College
1939 of Education.

1940 *Unit in the Social Studies* (with H. M. Long).

1941- Associate editor for The Macmillan Company.
1949

1942 Enlisted as apprentice seaman, United States Naval Reserve.

1944- Active duty in United States Naval Reserve in South
1945 Pacific; discharged in 1945 with rank of lieutenant commander.

1947 *Tales of the South Pacific* (Pulitzer Prize for Fiction).

1948 Divorced from Patti Koon; married Vange Nord.

1949 *The Fires of Spring;* play "South Pacific" opened on Broadway and ran for 1,925 performances.

1950 Awarded Doctor of Humane Letters, Rider College.

1951 *Return to Paradise; The Voice of Asia.*

1953 Named president of Asia Institute; *The Bridges at Toko-Ri.*

1954 Fund for Asia founded; awarded Doctor of Humane Letters, Swarthmore College; *Sayonara.*

1955 *The Floating World.*

1955 Divorced from Vange Nord; married to Mari Yoriko Sabusawa.

1956 Tour of Asia preparing television feature; covered Hungarian revolt.

1957 *The Bridge at Andau; Rascals in Paradise* (with A. Grove Day); *Selected Writings;* awarded Doctor of Laws, Temple University; awarded Doctor of Literature, American International College; appointed to Federal Advisory Arts Commission; plane ditched in Pacific off Iwo Jima (October).

1958 *The Hokusai Sketchbooks;* moved residence to Hawaii and active in Territorial elections.

1959 *Japanese Prints;* novel *Hawaii;* moved back to Bucks County.

1960 Active campaigning for John F. Kennedy in Presidential campaign.

1961 *Report of the County Chairman.*

1962 Campaigning as candidate for House of Representatives from Pennsylvania Eighth District (unsuccessful); writing script for musical comedy, "Tahiti"; *The Modern Japanese Print.*

1963 *Caravans;* most of year spent doing research in Israel.

James A. Michener

CHAPTER 1

Citizen of the World

UNTIL HE WAS FORTY, James Albert Michener had done almost everything except publish a book. His main apprenticeship came from adventuring in life rather than in growing up face to face with a typewriter.

Even to seek his own parentage was an adventure, a forlorn hope. The standard reference works solemnly state that the author was born on February 3, 1907, in New York City, son of Edwin and Mabel (Haddock) Michener. The father was a Quaker farmer of English extraction; the mother came from a North Ireland family settled near Wilmington, Delaware.

These books are in error.

"Although the extensive Michener clan has always welcomed me, and although I have appreciated their friendship and have maintained close association with them," James Michener recently told me, "I am not a Michener. I am not related to them. Actually, I do not know who my parents were, or where or when I was born. I never had a birth certificate. The problem became acute in 1931, when I wished to get a passport for travel in Europe. At that time my foster mother, Mabel Michener, took me to a local notary public and told him that I was a foundling whom she had taken care of since birth. The notary said I would not be able to get a passport on that statement, so in my presence he and my mother worked out a statement to the effect that I was the son of Edwin and Mabel (Haddock) Michener, and on these terms I got the passport.

"The same problem recurred in 1942 when I wished to enlist in the Navy. Again my mother testified that I was a foundling, and again it was found advisable to revert to the passport story, which was already in the government files. So again I became the son of Edwin Michener.

"The facts in the case are very clearly set forth in the official Michener family history.[1] This establishes that Edwin Michener was dead long before I was born. The date, locale and parentage of my birth I have never known."

Although near destitution herself, Mabel Michener, whom he always knew as his mother, took in waifs and raised them along with her own son, Robert. Six of her children went through high school, and three of them through college. Among these latter was the solemn-eyed James. His earliest recollections include lone trips to Philadelphia, where he was sent to pick up and deliver bundles of women's shirtwaists. Mabel Michener's chief income came from embroidering buttonholes in these shirtwaists.

I *From Poorhouse to the Pacific*

Jim grew up in dire poverty. When illness struck the family, he used to weather the bad times by moving into the county poorhouse near Doylestown. There, among sad-faced, bearded wrecks who shared a hoarded smear of margarine with him, Jim learned a sympathy for unfortunate people that was to color his whole attitude toward the world.

There were happy times, too, when he got off in a shady corner with a book (he does not remember when he learned to read), or paddled beneath a red, plank-covered bridge over the straggling Neshaminy Creek, hunting for hellgrammites to use for fish bait. He spent much time rambling around Bucks County, which lies northwest of Philadelphia—a county whose Indian, colonial, Quaker, and Pennsylvania Dutch history is reflected in such names as Perkasie, Washington's Crossing, Quakertown, and Trumbauersville (Levittown was a mass-housing development still in the future).

Jim went to Doylestown Grammar School, but at the age of fourteen he succumbed to the burning desire for travel that has never let him rest. He bummed his way around the United States, and in this way he saw every state except Washington, North Dakota, and Florida. On the road he enjoyed the food and friendship of some fifty families, whose hospitality made him an "incurable optimist" about human nature. On his return home he delivered newspapers, was a hotel watchman, wrote a sports column at the age of fifteen, and acted as a spotter of short-change "artists" at Willow Grove Park, an amusement center near Philadelphia, where, stationed near the bandstand, he became acquainted with John Philip Sousa and Victor Herbert.

Jim was graduated in 1925 from Doylestown High School, where he had been noted for prowess in basketball, baseball, tennis, and acting. Thanks to a flypaper memory that later was to bring him success as a world correspondent and interviewer, he maintained high marks in all his courses. A scholarship took him to Swarthmore College, a celebrated institution under Quaker auspices.

As a young student of art, Michener, like many others, burned with curiosity to view the celebrated collection of European paintings held privately in the guarded gallery of Dr. Albert Barnes, the terrible-tempered Philadelphia collector who had made his fortune through the patented eye remedy Argyrol. Michener wrote the doctor a letter from Pittsburgh, posing as a culture-struck steel-mill worker with an unpronounceable name. Garbed to fit the part, he was admitted to view the collection and even got a free lecture from its owner on the relationship between Matisse and Brahms.

During one summer vacation from college Michener joined the traveling tent shows of Chautauqua, that long-enduring institution of rural enlightenment which had first drawn crowds at the New York lake of that name in the 1870's. Young Jim's caravan was one of the last to tour the American countryside. One of his roles was leading man opposite pundit Drew Pearson's sister, in a teen-age vehicle called *Skidding*—it was from this play that the immensely popular Andy Hardy screen series was adapted. Michener's greasepaint experience on the road may well have increased his observation of dramatic techniques, although he is humble about his thespian powers.

Jim Michener graduated from Swarthmore in 1929, *summa cum laude,* with a Bachelor of Arts degree in English and in history. He was suspended several times "for girl troubles," but he won membership in Phi Beta Kappa, oldest of scholastic honor societies. He also served as Ivy Orator, with a wildly optimistic address on the subject of "On and Ever On," which he delivered not long before the stock market crash of 1929.

Young Michener chose the career of teacher, and throughout his life, although he has long since put his classroom service behind him, he has devoted much of his writing to informative purposes. Behind the novelist often lies the scholar, the editor, the professor.

For a while Michener served as master at Hill School, Pottstown, Pennsylvania. A traveling scholarship, the Lippincott Award, enabled him to make his first trip abroad. His headquarters were at gray, venerable St. Andrew's University in Scotland, but he also studied art at the British Museum in London and Sienese painting at Siena. From there he wandered to Salamanca in Spain, at whose ancient university he further studied the Renaissance and made friends with a troupe of bullfighters with whom he toured northern Spain. Later he shipped as chart-corrector on a Mediterranean collier. He is one of the few American authors holding papers as an able-bodied seaman in the British merchant marine. Before returning to his homeland, he also traveled up and down the Hebrides, helping to collect some of the rare songs and ballads remembered in those northern islands. His *wanderjahre* were also filled with a voracious reading of European authors.

When Michener returned to the United States, a salary of $1,200 during the depression years didn't look too bad. He taught from 1933 to 1936 at George School, a Quaker institution near Doylestown. In the latter year he gained a master's degree in teaching from the Colorado State College of Education at Greeley, on the staff of which he served as associate professor for the next three years.

Michener used to drive fifty-five miles to Denver to the Baker Federal Theater to see a Works Progress Administration repertory company perform the plays of Shaw, O'Neill, Sinclair Lewis, and others at a ticket cost of thirty-five cents. Here he continued his love affair with the American theater, until this activity of keeping actors on the federal payroll was abolished as a gigantic boondoggle. "Of all that Colorado has offered me, nothing was more important to my life than this theater," Michener says in justification for such federal support of creative people. "Somebody estimated the other day that on dramatic works that have been derived from my stories, the federal government has collected not less than ten million dollars in taxes, and on the personal income derived from them another twenty million dollars at least. . . . So for every dollar that the government 'wasted' in 1936, it got back $300 from me alone."[2]

Michener, who in all had attended nine universities in Europe and America, was visiting professor in the School of Education at Harvard University in 1940-41. Several years earlier he had begun his writing career in the educational press. Between 1936 and 1942 he published some fifteen articles "with lots of footnotes"; they were mainly concerned with teaching social studies in America's schools.

He is proudest, perhaps, of "The Beginning Teacher," chosen by the National Council for the Social Studies to lead off their tenth yearbook. His skill in making a story prove a point is shown in a short piece called "Who is Virgil T. Fry?" It is supposed to be told by the successor of a mysterious high-school instructor who had been condemned by all his colleagues and finally discharged by the school board, but who had been loved by all his students because he inspired them to learn much and to discuss their ideas freely. "Who is Virgil T. Fry?" first appeared in *Clearing House* in 1941; over the years it was twice reprinted therein, was printed twice by *Educational Digest,* and appeared also in *Scholastic* and in the *NEA Journal.* All these articles he, like the customary professor-writer, gave for publication without a nickel of payment; but, as he says, "I did learn how to write a sentence." This mastery of writing with clarity and popular appeal brought Michener the offer of a position in a textbook publishing house.

Anticipating conflict with the Axis powers, Michener published a warmly patriotic essay, "What Are We Fighting For?" one month before the United States was plunged into World War II. When the Japanese attacked Pearl Harbor on December 7, Michener was an editor in the offices of The Macmillan Company of New York. As a practicing member of the Society of Friends, he might well have been excused from serving in the armed forces. But he was a "fighting Quaker," like General Smedley Butler and Richard Nixon, and in 1942 he volunteered for service in the United States Navy.

Again his skill in writing brought him to the attention of superiors. He was sent to officers' training school; and, as a result of his European experience, he was given a special course qualifying him for carrier service in the Mediterranean theater. But his ability to draft reports brought about his assignment to

Washington. There he requested active duty. Interviewed by a lieutenant (junior grade), Michener was told, "You will be sent to the Pacific."

"I dislike seeming to be insubordinate," he responded, "but have you read the note at the bottom of my dossier, stating that I have been trained for Mediterranean service?"

"You will go to the Pacific!" repeated the officer. And thus, almost by chance, James A. Michener first went to the ocean that later was to become almost synonymous with his name.

II *Bus Ride to Random House*

Then began a wartime period of acting as super-secretary for aviation maintenance in the Solomon Islands and points north and south. As trouble-shooter and atoll-hopper, Michener was able to visit some fifty islands and to observe the activities that were to be narrated so authentically in *Tales of the South Pacific.* Freedom to enter many areas came, perhaps, because he did nothing to controvert the widespread idea that he was a relative of the powerful Vice-Admiral Marc A. Mitscher.

Then, as he relates, "A slack spell came and I was stranded on an island with nothing to do. Each afternoon I went up to a deep cacao plantation where I drafted outlines of some stories that had disturbed me. Each night I went to a big, empty building with a dozen mosquito bombs and typed out the material I had been thinking about." This was the beginning of his first novel.

Later Michener was assigned to flying duty and became senior naval historical officer for the area from New Guinea to Tahiti. While on this assignment he wrote extensive histories of naval operations ashore at Bora Bora and Tongatabu, of which he says: "Long after I'm dead somebody will find those histories gathering dust in Washington, and they'll be published as affectionate little records of the absurd." He has always made light of his accomplishments in uniform. "My war record was quite undistinguished and all I accomplished could have been done much better by a capable girl secretary, except for one week in Tahiti." Actually he was discharged from the navy with a fine battle record and the rank of lieutenant commander. He returned to the post of associate editor in the high school text division at Macmillan, where a brilliant future was promised him.

By the end of 1946, however, he had sold two of the South Pacific chapters to the *Saturday Evening Post*; and *Tales of the South Pacific* was published in February, 1947, under the imprint of his own house. This crucial event was marked by few people other than the author. The rare first edition of the *Tales* makes an odd item for collectors. Probably no future Pulitzer Prize book has ever appeared in a more sleazy format. The book was considered to have such slight hopes that the publisher used up an overstock of chalky paper whose surface was different on either side, and these pages were draped in a shoddy binding. New chapters were started right under the last line of the previous ones, and "Fo' Dolla'," which was to inspire one of the most successful musical comedies of our generation, began six lines from the bottom in order to conserve paper, thus saving a few dollars.

Contrary to popular belief, *Tales of the South Pacific* was never a best-seller. It sells today about the same number of copies annually that it did at the start. Orville Prescott of the daily New York *Times* was not the only reviewer to anticipate the high reading pleasure that was to come. Prescott's reception was to be warmly remembered by Michener; the review stated that *Tales* was "one of the best works of fiction yet to come out of the war . . . a substantial achievement which will make Mr. Michener famous. It is original in its material and point of view, fresh, simple and expert in its presentation, humorous, engrossing, and surprisingly moving . . . it is not primarily a book about combat and so deserves to escape from the present general dearth of interest in war books."[3]

On May 3, 1948, the Pulitzer Prize Committee at Columbia University gave a $500 award to *Tales of the South Pacific* as "a distinguished novel, preferably dealing with American life, by an American author." The book still caused no great stir and might have shared the quiet fate of such predecessors as *His Family* or *Years of Grace*. Luckily, Kenneth McKenna, an actor turned Hollywood motion picture executive, tried to sell Michener's book to his studio, but was told, "You could never make a picture out of this." To support his judgment, McKenna sent it to his brother Jo Mielziner, the famous stage designer, who took it to Richard Rodgers and Oscar Hammerstein II. They, as everyone knows, made it into the musical comedy *South Pacific,* which opened on Broadway in April, 1949, and ran for a total of 1,925 performances and which in its film version will run for years in many parts of the world.

"Two nights before their show opened," recalls Michener, "these men telephoned me. In addition to my royalty, which they were required to pay, they voluntarily gave me a part of the ownership, which they were not required to do and which I did not request. As a result, I was free to travel and to write as I pleased."

Michener remembered what sudden success had done to men like Thomas Heggen, who had committed suicide soon after his first novel, *Mr. Roberts,* had been well received. Michener determined to keep his head. The income from the musical show he reinvested in what he called "literary plant expansion." Assured for the first time of a modest living, he was able to write as he chose without regard for book markets.

His successive volumes showed that he was not content to spend his life writing and rewriting South-Seas fiction. Actually, they were amazingly varied. In succession he wrote (1) a travel volume in unique form—half hard reporting, half regional short stories; (2) a political book consisting of vignettes of Asian personalities; (3) an intense, bitterly controlled novel of the Korean War; (4) a novella of Japan in antique style; (5) a philosophical study of Japanese art; (6) a collaboration on biographies of ten violent and colorful characters from Pacific history; (7) a fiery report on the Russian suppression of the Hungarian revolt; (8) two other scholarly volumes of Japanese prints; (9) a voluminous novel of several generations in the lives of several racial groups in the Hawaiian Islands; (10) a report on the author's participation in the Kennedy campaign of 1960; and (11) a romantic travelogue about a group of Americans and Asians in 1947 in Afghanistan.

Freedom of choice and versatility of performance could hardly go farther than this. During all this period, Michener's most strenuous efforts were devoted to acting as a roving reporter for such magazines as *Life, Holiday,* and *Reader's Digest.* For these publications, the world was his beat. And his skill in writing developed more and more to the point where all his various endeavors paid generous rewards. His versatility also required fresh treatment by the reviewers of each new book. Since there was no such thing as "another typical Michener book," each had to be read and discussed.

His second novel, *The Fires of Spring,* is a tender story of growing up in America, a *Bildungsroman* if not a *Künstlerroman,* the type of semi-autobiographical work that it is customary for beginning writers to evolve. It was therefore surprising to be assured by Michener that not one word of it was written before he finished *Tales of the South Pacific.*

The Fires of Spring marked another crisis in the author's career. He had to change publishers. Macmillan, despite having a Pulitzer prizewinner on its staff, declined the second novel but not because of lack of merit. Michener had a future there as a senior editor, and it was amicably suggested to him that this did not include writing novels on the side. Michener chose to submit the manuscript to Random House, Inc. His action began an association which over the years grossed millions of dollars for that house. The acumen of the editorial team headed by Bennett Cerf under the Random imprint was well known in writing circles, but, typically, Michener's decision had a human rather than a calculated basis.

"I had visited the Random House offices," Michener once told me, "and had noted that their receptionist was a charming young Negro girl (she later appeared in the musical *Carmen Jones*). Most publishing houses at that time did not even employ Negroes in their shipping rooms. I imagined that Random's choice of a receptionist might cost some patronage, and I felt that an outfit willing to risk prejudice by such an act of faith would be a good one to associate with. So I got on a Fifth Avenue bus at Washington Square, rode up to 50th Street, and handed that Negro girl the manuscript of *The Fires of Spring.*"

III *Flight to the "Frenzied Fifties"*

Michener's appearance, at the summit of his Pulitzer and *South Pacific* fame, was that of a stocky fellow of medium height, with bespectacled, warm brown eyes; a placid Quaker smile; and one of the highest foreheads in modern American literature. He spoke slowly, precisely, in a voice like that of a teacher aiming at the back row of seats; and, at our first meeting, I was reminded that he had once been a professor of education. He kept in good physical shape, broke some amateur records for skin-diving in Hawaiian waters, and neither smoked nor drank (except for a friendly beer). He was at this time "returning to Paradise," accompanied by his second wife, to write a series of articles for *Holiday* magazine.

Michener's first marriage, to Patti Koon in 1935, had ended in divorce in 1948. In September of that year he had married twenty-six-year-old Vange A. Nord, a *Time Magazine* writer and an interior decorator. They lived in a flat at 85 Charles Street in Greenwich Village, on the walls of which were hung a Van Gogh print, an Italian Renaissance panel, and José Clemente Orozco's portrait of Emiliano Zapata.

As soon as it became financially possible, however, the Micheners acquired a forested hilltop acreage near Pipersville, twelve miles from his boyhood home at Doylestown. Bucks County had meanwhile become a fashionable refuge for such country gentry as Oscar Hammerstein, George S. Kaufman, Pearl Buck, S. J. Perelman, and Moss Hart; and Michener took pride in having been a "native" of that region. He and his wife designed a dwelling combining comfort and artistic charm, complete with swimming pool and caretaker's cottage.

Jim's job as a world reporter frequently interrupted construction. Work on a garage building was delayed when he was called upon to revisit the South Pacific for eight months. Back home again, he got the garage built; but before he could get his car into it the New York *Herald-Tribune* asked him to tour Asia on an assignment. Home once more, he started to paint the garage— but then a ten-thousand-mile lecture tour of the United States interfered.

Michener's knowledge of Asia brought him recognition and responsibilities. In April, 1953, the regents of the Asia Institute, the only graduate school in the United States then devoted exclusively to training in Asian affairs, named him president. Both he and James M. Landis, appointed as chancellor to succeed retiring founder Professor A. U. Pope, served without salaries, and an appeal for funds was issued to support the school, which had twenty-five candidates for the master's degree.

A year later, on February 7, 1954, Michener helped to found

the Fund for Asia, a national non-profit organization designed to provide technical aid in Asia by private agencies in the United States. He attended the Bandung Conference of non-Caucasian nations and spent several months in Afghanistan in 1955. He arrived in Afghanistan just as civil war seemed inevitable. When he reached the capital, national mobilization was announced, and for one terrifying moment it looked as if he was going to be one of the conscripts. For eleven weeks he lived in a land of tension; but Asia, he found, had somehow learned to solve its disputes short of war. In Saigon in July of that year, when demonstrators mobbed and pillaged his hotel, Michener was able to save his possessions from the rioters by announcing that he was an American and a friend.

The Fund for Asia lasted only two years; in December, 1956, Michener, as president, announced that it would end its activities because "recent world events in the Middle East and Hungary had made its discontinuance advisable."[4]

Working on a *Life* feature concerning the marriage of a G.I. and a Japanese girl, Michener was in Chicago in December, 1954. Two days before Christmas he attended a luncheon of friends of the Pfeiffer family and was introduced to Mari Yoriko Sabusawa, assistant editor of the American Library Association *Bulletin.* One of the first things she said to the author was that she didn't like the ending of *Sayonara.* An interracial marriage needn't always be a tragedy, she maintained.

Michener learned more about Mari. She had almost missed the luncheon because of another invitation. She had never been in Japan and could not read the language. She had lived in Chicago for a decade, working and studying political science at the University of Chicago. She had been born, however, in 1920 in Las Animas, Colorado. After the Pearl Harbor attack, she was one of the first Japanese-Americans to be sent to an internment camp in California, set up at the Santa Anita race track. She had preferred treatment: "I lived in Equipoise's stable." One of the first to be released, she went to Antioch College in Ohio, where classroom work is intertwined with practical experience on the job. And she ended the war in Washington doing top-secret work for the government.

Less than a fortnight after Michener met Mari, Vange Nord Michener sued for divorce on the grounds of "indignities" and complained that the writer was seldom home. The divorce was completed on the last day of August. She received custody of a Japanese boy that had been adopted by the childless couple.

James Michener and Mari Sabusawa were wed on October 23, 1955, in the Hilton Chapel at the University of Chicago. She was thirty-five; he, forty-eight. She was listed as Presbyterian, Michener as a Quaker; the minister was a Baptist. Newspapers commented that the bride did not greatly resemble the stately actress Hana-ogi of *Sayonara*: "Michener's bustling, bright-eyed American Madame Butterfly is neither tall nor exotic, has no theatrical background and cannot dance."

As a writer, Michener felt that this marriage would present no problems. "If I were a banker, say, in the South, I might encounter some difficulty." He predicted more such marriages, since the United States is becoming more and more international. Mari also felt that, since marriage is a personal thing, people who love each other should go ahead and marry. None of her relatives made objections. All her mother asked was: "Is he a good man? Will you be happy with him?"

The couple left for a honeymoon around the Pacific, passing through Hawaii on the way to Australia, where Michener had some writing assignments. Six months later, after a tour of East Asia, they returned via Hawaii. This time Michener, accustomed to travel with one seabag, arrived in Honolulu with his wife and thirty-eight pieces of luggage. He settled in his Waikiki apartment on the eighth floor of the Ainahau Apartments at 260 Lewers Road. He then began an intense collaboration with A. Grove Day on the completion of the volume called *Rascals in Paradise*.

One Saturday night in June, 1956, during a Honolulu Press Club dinner in his honor, Michener was presented by Admiral Felix Stump with the Navy Gold Cross, highest award given to a civilian and the first ever given to a writer, in recognition of his many services to the Navy.

In July, 1956, the Micheners went to the West Coast and drove across the country to Bucks County. By heavy use of air-mail facilities, the collaboration on the big biographical volume was finished.

Michener was soon back in Asia, on a task that few American authors had previously faced. He was asked by the National

Broadcasting Company to prepare a special ninety-minute television report called "Assignment—Southeast Asia." To make this color documentary, he traveled with camera crews for five weeks through Java, Bali, Malaya, Cambodia, Viet Nam, Thailand, and Burma. They interviewed fifteen major leaders, fifty or sixty personalities, and some three hundred anonymous men-in-the-street. Michener felt that presenting this film to the American public was harder than writing a book but that doing so had tremendous satisfactions.

In Amsterdam, homeward bound, he was asked by *Reader's Digest* to cover the Hungarian revolution which had erupted on October 23. The Russians had reoccupied the country on November 4, and the brutal suppression of the population was such a dramatic story that Michener was soon on his way to Vienna and to the bridge at Andau. He spent four weeks interviewing, day and night, hundreds of refugees and wearing out two interpreters. To see for himself the effects of Red domination, he accompanied Freedom Fighters on rescue expeditions, and helped people through the border swamps, across rivers and canals, and past false Austrian flags put up by the Russians to try to detour the fleeing Hungarians. Despite such hindrances, two hundred thousand of them escaped from tyranny, and Michener's resulting book was the first to document this international episode.

Early in 1957 Michener was given another global assignment—to write about the activities of the Strategic Air Command that protects the free world around the clock and around the world. In order to write about the men who fly the big nuclear bombing jets, Michener wanted to fly one himself; but an Air Force doctor, discovering a minor heart ailment resulting from the Hungarian episode, refused him permission to sit at the controls. Typically, Michener boarded a commercial plane to Honolulu, hunted up a medico who was a personal friend, obtained a clean bill of health, and soon had the thrill of piloting a Strategic Air Command bomber at forty thousand feet.

Since then, avoiding the temptation to be a cardiac cripple, he has skin-dived to a depth of sixty-five feet, traveled around the world four times, engaged in two major revolutions, explored the deserts of Central Asia and climbed the lower Himalayas, written four books, fought a couple of yearling bulls in Mexico, and played tennis nearly every Sunday—despite the perils of inevitable deterioration to be expected by a man in his "frenzied fifties."[5]

IV Best-Sellers and Politics

In the first half of 1957, Michener had three books on the stands: *The Bridge at Andau*, the *Rascals in Paradise* collaboration completed the previous year, and *Selected Writings*, a Modern Library anthology. In June he was awarded two honorary degrees: a Doctor of Laws from Temple University and a Doctor of Letters from the American International College. In October he was appointed by Secretary of State John Foster Dulles to a Federal Advisory Arts Commission.

An unsought adventure came to Michener early in October, 1957. He and twelve others took off in a C-47 transport from the plateau airfield of Iwo Jima, a stop on his trip from Guam to Japan. Almost at once, one of the engines conked out and the other began to falter. The plane crashed into a heavy sea at eighty-five knots and sank in three minutes. During this time the occupants had quickly boarded a life raft. A small boat sent to pick them up had its engine fail a mile away from the drifting raft. The castaways paddled closed to the rescue launch but without making contact. Finally a Japanese sailor tied a rope around his waist and swam from the launch, through shark-ridden waters, to the raft, where he was pulled in with a great deal of hearty affection. No lives were lost. At the time of the crash, Michener, seeing the smallness of the raft, abandoned all his possessions, including the manuscript of *Hokusai's Manga*, which was to have been published in Japan, and a fat book of notes for a novel which he had been considering writing about Hawaii.

James Michener changed his residence in 1958 from Pennsylvania to Hawaii, but Mari kept hers in Bucks County because she wanted them to call that area their home. Settled with Mari in Waikiki, he began work, in consultation with research assistant Mrs. Clarice B. Taylor, on his most voluminous book, the gigantic novel on Hawaii. He started the final writing of this long-planned book on May 1 and worked at it steadily for ten months. He did not leave the islands during this time except for a four-day appearance at the Pan-Pacific Festival in San Francisco.

Michener enjoyed the tail-flapping freedom of the Hawaiian "aloha shirt," but he aroused some hostility when he attacked the shapeless *muumuu,* the enveloping Mother Hubbard deriving from old missionary days when the female natives were covered up with bright flowered prints. "You can't tell what's under all that calico," Michener grumbled. "It's Hawaii's answer to carbohydrates."

Despite his daily labors at his writing table, Michener plunged into local politics. He had forsaken his many years as a staunch Republican and become a peacemaker in the faction-ridden Democratic party of the islands. His old fascination with sociology and politics drove him to attend dozens of coffee parties and rallies complete with flower leis and hula dancers. His strong advocacy of statehood for Hawaii had made him influential, and the liberalism which had caused him to shift to Adlai Stevenson in 1956 led him to see in the Democrats of Hawaii the champions of the underdog. He traveled to islands other than Oahu in 1959 and strongly pleaded for the election of John A. Burns for governor several days after Burns himself had decided that he could not win. (Burns did achieve the governorship in the Democratic landslide of 1962.)

Michener's Republican friends were puzzled by his advocacy of a party that seemed to them recklessly trying to destroy the new state that was undergoing its first election—some of them felt that he was swayed by his wife. The ending of the novel *Hawaii* presents the outcome of an election as Michener would have wished it. The reality was the election of Republicans as governor and lieutenant-governor, with a bare majority of Republicans in the state Senate to offset a big majority of Democrats in the House. A series of five articles that Michener wrote for the Honolulu *Star-Bulletin,* including one with the title of "How to Lose an Election," is an outspoken post-mortem by Michener the realistic political scientist.

In the spring, with his novel *Hawaii* finished, Michener shipped aboard a sailboat which was beating its way back from Honolulu to Los Angeles, following its participation in the biennial trans-Pacific yacht race. The writer told himself that, since he had written so much about the Pacific, he should cross it in a small vessel to see what it was like at close quarters. He found out. The yacht took twenty-two days of buffeting, with the rail under water most of the trip. It was a tedious, wet passage; and even the professionals were seasick.

On land again, he and Mari drove across the country and found not much improvement in conditions. "We did strike very bad weather driving home and on the stretch from Wichita to Kansas City were on a sleet-covered highway where we did about ten miles an hour all day," he wrote me. "It was rather harrowing but interesting to be back in the middle of weather as weather should be." The couple might well have yearned for Hawaii, but some time would pass before they could return. Christmas was spent in Mexico, for Michener was doing a piece about bullfighters.

In November the novel *Hawaii* had been published. Even before this novel, some six million copies of Michener's books had been sold in twenty-four languages. At once the new novel hit the best-seller lists and stayed at or near the top for no less than twenty months. Even before publication, the film rights were sold for $600,000 against a ten per cent share in the gross— the highest price ever paid for a picture property.

During the following summer, Michener diverted himself by playing the type-cast role of "the perfesser" in a production of *South Pacific* at New Hope, Pennsylvania. He also began campaigning for the election of John F. Kennedy for the Presidency of the United States, an experience to be related in *Report of the County Chairman.*

V A Million Dollars to Spare

A furor arose in Honolulu in April, 1961, when an interview with Michener reprinted from the New York *Post* quoted his amplification of a paragraph in the forthcoming book. He had mentioned three reasons why he had decided to leave Hawaii and return to his residence in Pennsylvania. Among these was the statement that, despite Hawaii's great achievements in racial harmony, "on the day-to-day operating level at which my wife and I had to live, we met with more racial discrimination in Hawaii than we did in eastern Pennsylvania, and my wife understandably preferred to live permanently in the latter place."[6]

Queried by transatlantic telephone in Seville, Spain, where he was working at the time, Michener stated that he would still like to return to Hawaii some day and that the decision to leave came from himself and not from his wife. A letter of amplification from Michener to Clarice Taylor, which was published in Honolulu in July, helped slightly to put the misunderstanding into its proper place, but the passions of many good people in Hawaii, most of whom had not read the novel nor *Report of the County Chairman*, were slow to cool.

In November, 1959, Michener had denied to reporters the rumor that he intended to run on the Democrat ticket for governor of Hawaii the following year. Anticipating the local irritation that might be caused by *Hawaii*, he warned his would-be electorate: "I feel that writers do not make good elected officials because writers have to probe into so many aspects of community life—and when they do, they are bound to make more enemies than friends."[7] However, within the next two years he found himself back in Pennsylvania, about which he had *not* written; and he changed his mind about participation. During nine months in 1962 Michener devoted most of his waking hours to campaigning as a Democrat for a seat in the United States Congress from Pennsylvania's Eighth District.

His motives were explained in an article he wrote for the *Saturday Evening Post*:

> On the surface, I would seem to be the least likely candidate for public office that a major party could find. But three significant factors didn't appear on the surface. (1) I used to teach American history and took the subject very seriously. (2) I have lived in many foreign nations that did not have good government, and I have come to respect self-government as one of the highest attainments of man. (3) As a boy I lived in dire poverty and was rescued by scholarships, fellowships, and the generosity of our nation. I owe a debt to America which is constantly in my mind and which I have always been willing to repay, either by volunteering for military service or by helping out in government. . . .
>
> I'm running for one of the 435 most important jobs in the United States and the opposition has a right to belt me with every fact they can turn up. They won't say anything worse than book reviewers have said in the past.[8]

Michener's experience in the rough-and-tumble of politics in Hawaii had prepared him well for the strenuous job of fighting for a Pennsylvania seat that had been held by Republicans for twenty-six years. His opponent had been re-elected twice, but Michener and his wife did not yield to tradition. They zigzagged around Bucks and Lehigh counties in a small station wagon, attending union picnics, clambakes, book club meetings, Pennsylvania-Dutch tall-story contests, dedications of new firehouses, and various coffee hours, asking for votes. Michener found that many people were curious about meeting his Japanese-American wife; and, when they did so, they often decided to vote for her husband. And he was frequently diverted on the stump by questioners who wanted to ask him about his novel *Hawaii*. "I'm going to charge the Hawaii Visitor's Bureau half of my campaign expenses," he joked, following a session at a ladies' tea party. "Four-fifths of them told me they had read the book and wanted to climb on the first boat available to the islands."[9] But political experts who had predicted that Michener could win only by a miracle were proved correct. However, when he lost by only 17,000 votes, he could feel that his months of effort had not proved fruitless.

During the hot political campaign Michener also found time to work in collaboration with various Broadway people on a musical comedy, "Tahiti," based on some of his earlier work. He also continued his interest in art by using writing income to purchase canvases of contemporary American painters. In May, 1961, he attended an exhibition of sixty of his acquisitions at a gallery in Little Rock, Arkansas. One hundred of them were shown in Allentown, Pennsylvania, in 1962. He built an additional room on his Bucks County home to display his paintings, most of which will eventually be permanently housed as gifts to American museums.

Michener's position as one of the best-paid writers alive raises the question of his attitude toward money and the creative person. As a poor boy who had often been broke, he grew up unworried by lack of financial security. "I have always insisted that the writer be properly paid for his labors, like anyone else," he told me recently. "But what he does with his earnings, after taxes, is his own affair. I don't think this attitude is inconsistent." On the other hand, few writers are more generous in writing for low fees to oblige a friend or to help a good cause. He will work just as hard on an essay for which he gets nothing as he will on the highest-paying assignment. He gave away a series of Korean War dispatches which were headlined around the world. His three volumes on Japanese prints cost him a large amount of money to publish, and all proceeds from a new fourth volume on contemporary Japanese artists, which sells at $150 a copy, will go to the artists themselves.

"Yes, what we do with money is our privilege," he repeated. "Not long ago Mari and I sat down and calculated that our assets, not counting royalties in escrow, amounted to just about a million dollars. It's silly for two people to be responsible for having all that cash around. We decided to give it all away. To whom? Well, the money came from the arts. Logically, it should go back to the arts. And it will."

CHAPTER *2*

Start in the South Pacific

MICHENER'S FIRST BOOK, *Tales of the South Pacific*, was published early in 1947; it won the Pulitzer Prize for fiction for that year. The book retains the freshness of having been written on the spot at about the time of the action it relates, but the author tried to present the scene as it would be remembered in the future. "I wrote that book under extremely difficult circumstances," he recalls. "I was in the Navy on Espíritu Santo in the South Seas. The mosquitoes drove me batty and the humidity was terrible. It took me a year and a half. . . . I was sure the people who were bitching so much about the Islands would not remember them that way. I try to anticipate history."[1]

Although never a best-seller, *Tales of the South Pacific* was quite favorably received by the reviewers. In the Sunday edition of the New York *Times*,[2] David Dempsey called it "truly one of the most remarkable books to come out of the war in a long time. . . . The book's only weakness—the interminable length of some of the tales. Mr. Michener saw so much, and his material is so rich, that he simply could not leave anything out. . . . Fortunately, even when he is uneconomical, Mr. Michener is never dull. Nor is his lengthiness always a fault." Orville Prescott, who had been enthusiastic in the daily New York *Times,* was even more so in the *Yale Review*: "These *Tales of the South Pacific* are magnificently entertaining. But they are more than that. Mr. Michener is an acute observer of human character. An adroit literary artist, a man with a philosophy of life which makes him tolerant of many human weaknesses but not of all, he is certainly one of the ablest and one of the most original writers to appear on the American literary scene for a long time."[3]

Michener has modestly stated that the Pulitzer Prize came to him in 1947 because there was no competition and that he would not have won it in any other year.[4] This idea is not borne out by the facts: the year 1947 saw also the publication of Laura Hobson's *Gentleman's Agreement*, John Steinbeck's *The Pearl* and *The Wayward Bus*, Sinclair Lewis' *Kingsblood Royal*, Vincent McHugh's *The Victory*, David Davidson's *The Steeper Cliff*, Theodore Dreiser's *The Stoic*, John Horne Burns's *The Gallery*, A. B. Guthrie's *The Big Sky*, and Malcolm Lowry's *Under the Volcano*. In the minds of the judges there must have been a good deal of competition, particularly to cause them to choose for the first time "a book of short stories," as the New York *Times* reported, "even such related short stories as make up Mr. Michener's excellent book."[5]

Michener himself has always thought of the book as a novel because a strong theme and a changing but limited setting around the Pacific islands lend unity and because among the large cast are several recurring figures, especially Tony Fry, Bus Adams, and the narrator himself.[6] The nineteen chapters are also tied together by the giant anti-Japanese operation—called "Alligator" in the book—which slowly rises into a crescendo and a climax, and has its aftermath in the cemetery at Hoga Point.

It is true that the focus of narration sometimes shifts,[7] but this is the case with other books too. If *Moby Dick* is a novel, and it is, so is *Tales of the South Pacific*.

I *Progeny of the "Bounty"*

Appreciation of Michener's first novel is increased if one studies the various chapters as the story unrolls. The opening sketch, "The South Pacific," stresses the beauties of the region to which war had come, as well as the differences between it and other theaters, such as Europe. For several years it was to be a war of waiting, "timeless, repetitive waiting." But it was also a war in which people were important—such as Bloody Mary, who sold dried human heads as souvenirs, and the old native who persuaded the Americans to let him make a parachute jump, and thereafter lived silent, a being apart. Especially were the American servicemen in the foreground of the picture: the mad commander who would summon a carpenter at two in the morning to sandpaper the floor of his hut; Admiral Bull Halsey, who grunted out during a defeat, "We'll be in Tokyo by Christmas!"; Admiral Millard Kester, a fictional creation whom we first see tearing off his pants and being immobilized by a jammed zipper; and Tony Fry, everybody's friend, whose old TBF, used in missions for ferrying liquor, had twelve beer bottles painted on its side. In three pages, the general tone of the stories to come is adumbrated.

The second piece, "Coral Sea," tries to reveal the significance of this ·battle during which the Japanese fleet was first turned back and the shores of Australia and New Zealand were rescued by American naval might from the shadow of invasion by a cruel enemy. This action, truly one of the decisive battles of history, is still annually celebrated in Australasia in a way that overwhelms visiting Americans, who for the first time begin to understand the deep feeling of gratitude for their salvation that our allies are glad to express.

But Michener avoids the temptation to offer a standard battle description here. The meaning of the trembling victory comes most significantly to an isolated group of allied airmen who are stuck in a malarial, bombed-out swamp on Vanicoro, with a portable radio receiver their only contact with the action. Of all the men, this crisis is most desperate for Leftenant Grant, a silent New Zealander whose rickety PBY has finally crashed in the bay and left him grounded. His wife back home has volunteered to mobilize other women with axes and pick handles to defend their menaced beaches. For three days, Grants sits silent at the radio. Then, when the great news comes through, he presents his surviving comrades with a bottle of Scotch; and, after a few fumbling words of a speech of celebration, he falls over—dead drunk.

One of the best stories about the Pacific ever written is "Mutiny." To Norfolk Island, a tiny dot between New Zealand and Noumea, is sent the narrator, the "I" of *Tales of the South Pacific*, who is not necessarily Michener himself. He has been sent by Admiral Kester to find out what is holding up a vital operation—the leveling of an airstrip that will be the only salvation of the supply planes flying between Australasia and New Caledonia to prepare for the Guadalcanal campaign.

A decision that should be made in an hour drags on for weeks. There is only one logical spot for the runway—but it happens to be the one spot that is covered by a two-mile avenue of towering Norfolk pines which had been planted "because God has been kind in His wisdom to bring us here" by descendants of the *Bounty* mutineers settled on this far isle. Tony Fry, charged with giving the order to bulldoze the strip, has apparently been led from his simple duty by the pleas of the Norfolk inhabitants, including Lucy, a simple-minded girl, and white-haired old Teta Christian, descendant of the man who had led the mutiny against Captain Bligh on the *Bounty*.

Profoundly, Michener uses history to reinforce the theme of his tale. Norfolk was one island in the Pacific never reached by man until Captain James Cook set foot there. It was later a prison island for the murderous hard cases that even the penal colony of Australia could not subdue; the impressive stone walls of the buildings erected by convict laborers were topped with broken glass to protect the jailers from the attacks of mutinous convicts. After the final mutiny, the island was emptied and then offered to the *Bounty* people who were invited to emigrate from their Pitcairn hideaway. And at the dénouement, when the narrator—bemused like Fry into a delay to avoid destroying "the loveliest monument in the South Pacific," "a living cathedral" of unique, giant trees—is forced at last to issue the order for their destruction, Tony Fry in a gesture of defiance dynamites one of the bulldozers and credits the two women with its ruin. In this isle of mutiny, even an American naval officer reverts to passion and rebellion and takes a stand against the destruction that authority has decreed. Ironically, at the end, the lovely trees are blasted down; but not one of the grim, empty buildings of the penal settlement has had to be destroyed.

One of the tales from the Pacific war that Michener did not use concerns the interrogation of a Japanese prisoner. Asked which men were best at jungle fighting, he replied: "Japanese." For second best: "Australians." When asked about Americans, he answered: "Americans no jungle fighters. Cut jungle all down." "Mutiny" reveals the reluctance of at least one American to engage in the brutal, bulldozer sort of war that had to be used against the Japanese aggressors.

"An Officer and a Gentleman" is handsome Ensign Bill Harbison, a college athlete from the mountain states and the husband of a Vassar girl. Stuck for months in a soft job as recreation officer on Efate, unable to obtain promotion ahead of the slow navy system, and unable to transfer to a theater of action, Bill has his main character traits revealed by the omniscient narrator. Competently doing his work in less than an hour a day, Bill spends his time writing to his wife, exercising his body, and relaxing his mind until the day when the nurses arrive. Then, starved for women's society, he first displays his "mother-complex" by dating Dinah Culbert. She enjoys the attention while it lasts, but remarks: "I pity the next girl he goes with!"

II *She Finds Her a Wonderful Guy*

The next girl is Nellie Forbush, later to be the heroine of the musical play *South Pacific*. She is a small-town girl, and she realizes the irony of the situation in which navy nurses find themselves. They are classed as officers but can seldom find their equals among the male officers. "Cut off by law from fraternizing with those men who would like to marry them and who would have married them in civilian life, they find their friendships restricted to men who are surprisingly often married or who are social snobs" (47).

The joys of dating on a romantic island in the tropics when war is at a standstill and passions are free to rove have their expected outcome. At the climax, Bill's snobbishness is nakedly revealed: "The damned girl was proposing to him! What was happening here? He swallowed hard and looked at her, a common little girl from some hick town. . . . He knew Nellie was his for the asking, but damn it all she was nothing but a little country girl. Hell, he wouldn't look at her twice in the States" (51). On the way back to his quarters, he feels a thin line of fat menacing his athletic stomach: "Soft living. I better get back to kicking that football in the afternoon."

"The Cave" is an exploration of the meaning of courage. Three men are contrasted in the story. One is Lieutenant Commander Charlesworth, an Annapolis graduate, and the skipper of one of the PT boats at the Tulagi base who are trying with feeble, brave little vessels of plywood to fight off the big Japanese ships that menace the American forces on Guadalcanal. A second is Lieutenant Tony Fry, the reservist who arrives with plenty of whiskey and snuggles down in a cosy hangout inside a cave commanding a view of The Slot. Fry, to whom humanity is the most precious thing, jeers at navy protocol and confesses frankly his fear of death; but night after night he drags himself down to the dock and boards Charlesworth's frail craft "to see what the heroes are doing" and to duel with Jap destroyers. The heroes are busy holding a defensive line against suicidal odds, and Charlesworth is one of the bravest of them all.

Fry's mission is to receive the radio messages of a volunteer coast-watcher, an exiled Britisher who flits from island to island for two long months, risking betrayal and death daily in order to send revealing weather reports and observations of Japanese troop and plane movements. "The Remittance Man," as he humbly calls himself, is merely a Malaita trader who has married a Melanesian wife and who, for no sound motive that Fry can figure out, is living every moment with a fear balanced only by the all-embracing importance of his messages to the allied battlers on Guadalcanal. He is the third of the men who must face and solve the problem of how to crawl out of his deep spiritual dugout, day after bloody day, and face the terror.

"And so," remarks the narrator, now attached to Charlesworth's staff, "arguing about the Remittance Man, we studied ourselves and found no answers" (64). What keeps Fry interested is the question of the power that holds the Remittance Man on his job, although courting certain death. Even when the gruesome details of that death have been ascertained by the navy men on a crazy submarine scouting expedition, the question still remains. At the end, even Charlesworth, who has won three medals for superhuman bravery against Japanese ships, speculates on the personal history of the Britisher whose sign-off words, "Good hunting, Americans!", has led the way to the evacuation of Guadalcanal by the beaten Japanese. The theme of the story is related to the title:

> How does any man have the courage to go to war? . . . And I hated Tony Fry for having raised such questions. I wanted to shout at him, "Damn it all! Why don't you get out of the cave?

Why don't you take your whiskey bottles and your lazy ways and go back to Noumea?" . . . And then I understood. Each man I knew had a cave somewhere, a hidden refuge from war. For some it was love for wives and kids back home. . . . For others the cave consisted of jobs waiting, a farm to run, a business to establish, a tavern on the corner of Eighth and Vine. For still others the cave was whiskey, or wild nights in the Pink House at Noumea, or heroism beyond the call of valor.

(72)

And for Tony and Charlesworth, their "cave" was the contemplation of the courage of another man. "The Englishman's great courage in those critical days of The Slot buoyed their equal courage" (73). For those who today may have to face a greater Guadalcanal, "The Cave" is still a heartening parable.

"The Milk Run" is told to Tony Fry by Lieutenant Bus Adams, a naval bomber pilot. Anything but a peaceful, routine mission is his trip to Munda. The thrill of an authentic adventure northwest of Guadalcanal is conveyed in offhand tones, complete with accurate flyer talk. Shot down in the bay at seven-thirty in the morning, without even a life raft, Bus Adams is a sitting duck for a Japanese bullet. But, miraculously, he is protected for five hours by a circling cover of New Zealand and American aircraft. His rescue becomes a point of honor with Admiral Kester and the focus of a side battle in the war. Lieutenant Grant, the New Zealand flyer, lands his PBY next to Bus and takes him aboard. But at once the plane's wing is shot away, and all the men are in the water. Grant, protagonist of the "Coral Sea" chapter, remarks mournfully: "Second PBY I've lost since I've been out here." The windup of the affair preserves the life of Bus Adams at an estimated cost to the taxpayer of some $600,000. But as Bus remarks: "It's sure worth every cent of the money. If you happen to be that pilot."[8] To Americans, even in wartime, human life is precious.

"Alligator" is an interchapter with little story content. It foreshadows the big push for which all the painful waiting is a prelude. "Alligator" is the code name for this gigantic operation, and the audacity of the decision to attack Kuralei, a thousand miles northward behind enemy lines, is presented in factual prose. The narrator is the man selected by chance to carry from Pearl Harbor to Noumea, in a locked and guarded briefcase, the bulky mimeographed orders for the operation in which men would die or not die, families would be bereft, and women would or would not marry. "The intensity, the inevitability, the grind-ingness of Alligator were too great for any one man to comprehend" (93).

"Our Heroine" is Ensign Nellie Forbush, later to be glorified on Broadway by Mary Martin. After her sad affair with Bill Harbison, she asks to be transferred to an island to the north; and there she meets the charming Emile De Becque, the prototype of Ezio Pinza. The view from his hilltop is a delight to the girl from a small town near Little Rock, Arkansas,[9] and so is the view from the secluded pavilion in his cacao grove. She discovers that he left France because he had stabbed a local bully to death, but she listens to his proposal. Emile is all man, a leader of the French community and, as Bus Adams casually reveals to Nellie, a hero with the island women. In fact, he has no less than eight lovely but illegitimate daughters.

The shock of having her future husband the father of eight girls younger than herself affects Nellie less than the realization that the girls are not all white. Four of them are half Javanese; two, half Tonkinese; and two others, half Polynesian. "Emile De Becque, not satisfied with Javanese and Tonkinese women, had also lived with a Polynesian. A nigger! To Nellie's tutored mind any person living or dead who was not white or yellow was a nigger. And beyond that no words could go!" (111-12).

The fact that Emile had not married because he dreamed that some day Nellie would come to the island and be the mistress of his household cannot offset the shock. But on the way back to the hospital in his jeep, Emile defends her from four lurking American rapists. Charlie Benedict, back in Otolousa, Arkansas, doesn't have a chance against Emile. Nellie had left home to see the world and meet people, and she had come at the right time to the right place. "Out here," counsels her friend Dinah Culbert, "good people seem to get better and bad people get worse." And Nellie's mind is changed. "I got me a man!" she says joyously. Racial prejudice has been overcome by love. And the eight step-daughters are lovely.

III   *Boars' Teeth and Religion*

It is not only a fighting war but a waiting war. In "Dry Rot," Joe, the shoemaker from Columbus, Ohio, wants only to serve his time and keep out of trouble. For twenty-seven months on a frizzling coral atoll west of the Solomons, he fights off the temptation to go rock-happy. He survives the tortures of jungle fungus and peeling skin, lack of whiskey and even water, and monotonous duty; but, after Luther Billis passes through and adopts the lonely sailor, Joe is able even to enjoy the beauties of moonlight on the Pacific shore. The new skipper manages to give Joe a chance to take a free nip of whiskey now and then, and life seems glorious when Billis the SeaBee manages to fix up Joe with a lovely pen pal, Alice Baker. Joe is about to mail his picture to Alice when the tragic news of her death arrives. "I got to get out of here!" is the sailor's desperate decision. Twenty-seven months is too long a time to fight off the screaming meemies.

The longest story in the book—and one of the three main sources for the musical play—is "Fo' Dolla'." In it we meet the memorable Bloody Mary; her slight, shy daughter Liat; and big, virile marine lieutenant Joe Cable. But first we meet Atabrine Benny, philosophizing druggist from Waco, Texas, who travels around the islands administering anti-malarial pills to all the civilians. On a jeep ride with Benny, the narrator first encounters the redoubtable Mary, an indentured laborer from Tonkin, China: "She was, I judge, about fifty-five. She was not more than five feet tall, weighed about 110 pounds, had few teeth and those funereally black, was sloppy in dress, and had thin ravines running out from the corners of her mouth. These ravines, about four on each side, were usually filled with betel juice, which made her look as if her mouth had been gashed with a rusty razor. Her name, Bloody Mary, was well given" (139).

With an oval, yellow face and with almond eyes beneath a peachbasket hat, Mary is sly and aggressive; but people are fond of her. She is an even bigger "dealer" than Luther Billis. She can sell a grass skirt, dyed with atabrine pills, for "fo' dolla'," and she sells a shrunken human head for fifty. With a volley of foul language taught her by idle soldiers, she can vanquish all the military police on the island. But her first sight of Joe Cable leads her to an unwonted subjection to orders because she starts at once to do her best to obtain Joe as an American son-in-law.

Thereafter we follow Joe Cable's emotions as he makes his first, rhapsodic visit to Bali-ha'i. This little island, just off Vanicoro, is a Michener invention. Bali-ha'i has passed into our language as a symbol for the island of all our dreams: "Like a jewel, it could be perceived in one loving glance. It was neat. It had majestic cliffs facing the open sea. It had a jagged hill to give it character. It was green like something ever youthful, and it seemed to curve itself like a woman into the rough shadows formed by the volcanoes on the greater island of Vanicoro" (147-48). Bali-ha'i is a refuge on which have been collected all the South Pacific women who might be insulted by rude G.I.'s: bare-breasted Gauguin girls of Polynesia, high-heeled French ladies, nuns of the hospital staff—and Liat.

The idyllic, impossible love affair of the officer from Philadelphia and the slim Tonkinese virgin is told at length—and with many variations on the theme of interracial tension. The story must be long because the increasing frenzy of Cable and the impossibility of their marriage must develop like a lingering illness. Desperate with passion, Cable forgets his work and sees his sweetheart again and again: but, as time runs out, it becomes tragically clear that Joe, even if he has thrown over his Bryn Mawr fiancée, cannot marry Liat. She is cold-heartedly sold by Bloody Mary to Benoit, the sloppy, lustful French plantation owner. And Joe Cable is summoned to embark on the big push that will, we suspect, lead him to glory and the cemetery at Hoga Point.

While they waited and worked, the men in the Pacific thought of their wives at home and wrote to them letters revealing a variety of personalities. In "Passion" we are given three kinds of love letters. One is from a naïve young sailor with a strong libido, who frankly exchanges nostalgic letters with his wife that could get them both arrested. Dr. Paul Benoway, the meditative medico of LARU-8, who has just survived the crash of a flying boat and four days of sizzling torture on a life raft, tries to write to his wife about this highest adventure of his life. "On the fourth day," he says, with unwonted lyricism, "when I saw the sun again, I felt like an Aztec's human sacrifice who waits at the end of the fiftieth year to see whether or not the sun will rise. Like him, I knew that when the sun rises again the world is saved and there is still hope. But like the Aztec I also knew that with the rising of the flaming beacon my individual torture would begin" (190-91). His words sound phoney, and he tears up the paragraph.

But later, as a censor, he reads the letter of Lieutenant Bill Harbison. Bill has written up their raft experience as if it were a yarn from *War Aces* in order to make himself appear to be the perfect lover as well as the heroic pilot. Benoway yields to temptation, and copies into his own letter two pages from the flyer's passionate screed. But it doesn't sound like the pedestrian style of the good doctor himself; it seems silly. He tears up the plagiarized pages and sends his original epistle, signed "All my love, Paul."

"A Boar's Tooth" is a story about religion. Luther Billis gets Tony Fry interested in the lovely ivory bracelets made from the curved tusks of the Melanesian boars raised by the savages in their villages on the volcanic slopes. Billis describes the sacred pigs:

> "All their lives they live in that little circle, tied to the tree. . . . The last four years must be real painful."
> "Four years?"
> "Yeah, it takes about seven years to grow a good tusk. It begins to enter the face about the fourth year. This here pig lived about five years after the tusks started through the bone."
> "How horrible!" Fry said.
> "Seems funny to me," Billis said. "But everyone I show this to always thinks about the pig. What about the people? They was mighty proud of this porker. It was the best pig in the area. It was sacred."
>
> (209, 211)

That night, Fry is drawn into an argument with a soured fellow officer about the sacred-pig religion. Fry says:

> "Pain is at the center of all religions. Almost all beauty, too. Fine things, like human beings, for example, are born of pain. Of great suffering. Of intense, in-driving horror. Fine things

never come cheaply. . . . Here you are, staked out on a jungle island. . . . What holds you fellows here? A three-foot chain to the stake of custom? . . . I think there must be something ennobling in this vast and timeless waste. Not to me, but to somebody who follows me. . . . Well, fifty years from now somewhere. . . . Let's say in Des Moines, Iowa—some high school girl will suddenly catch a faint intimation of what we accomplished out here."

(212-13)

The "big dealer" Billis promotes a trip from Espíritu Santo to Vanicoro to see a special pig-killing celebration. In the party is little Chaplain Jones. On the way to the island in the crash boat, the chaplain gives a lecture on the religion of the Santa Cruz group: "I don't know of anything in the world quite like this pig worship. . . . Primarily it's a monument to man's perversity. There is no place on earth where living is so easy as on these islands. . . . But there was one flaw. Amid all this luxury there was no reason for living. . . . They created, at one swoop, something to live for. Now believe me when I tell you that they took one of the commonest things in their acquaintance, one of the dirtiest: a jungle pig" (214-15).

No detail is omitted of the ceremony at which the pigs are clubbed to death and carefully butchered. Dr. Benoway gets sick at the sight. The most perfect of pigs—his tusks had made two complete circles, burrowing for years twice through the pig's living face and once through the jawbone—is killed and his tusks are given as souvenirs, one to Fry and the other to the chaplain. The chaplain gives his away to the doctor, saying: "The appurtenances of the religion are slightly revolting." Fry laughs: "I feel that way myself, sometimes, on Sunday in Connecticut" (222).

IV *"You Didn't Know What War Was"*

"Wine for the Mess at Segi," a story of a Pacific Christmastide, reveals the secret of how Tony Fry got his liquid refreshments. He and Bus Adams take a last ride in the antiquated plane christened the "Bouncing Belch" (ordinarily used to ferry beer cases), along with the unnamed narrator, who now returns and incidentally reveals himself as a Harvard graduate (Fry the wangler is from Yale).

The crazy odyssey of the trio covers thousands of miles, from the Jap-held Shortlands group in the north to New Caledonia in the south, where the battered flyers, on their way home with twenty-two cases of prime whiskey, visit the four beautiful De Becque sisters. The final-landing decision that Bus Adams has to make—with Tony, the liquor, and a traded washing machine in the bomb-bay—results in the destruction of the "Belch" but in a hearty Christmas party for the Segi mess. Their Christmas present from the skipper is the news that they have been chosen to hit the next beachhead. Their shout of thanks can be heard half a mile away along the shore.

"The Airstrip at Konora" is a hymn of praise to the SeaBees, the Construction Battalions of civilians who could do anything from mending a zipper to constructing a landing field on a crooked little Pacific atoll under enemy fire. Big Commander Hoag, a contractor from Georgia, is untinged with the prejudices that would keep lesser officers from getting the most out of their working teams. Ordered to build the field that will be the main steppingstone toward the capture of Kuralei, he is also charged with putting down the airstrip in fifteen days after the landing of the marines.

Hoag is able to handle not only modern machinery but men like Lieutenant Pearlstein, who detects the possibility that a hidden ravine on the atoll might threaten disaster and who, once proved right, is given the job of filling in the ravine with equipment that is put out of action again and again. Hoag has to manage SeaBees like Luther Billis, who will volunteer to make a suicidal night landing on occupied Konora to spy out the land and who shortly after will go AWOL—disappearing for two days to win a bet and coming back with two captured samurai swords as souvenirs.

The story is also about the importance of coral in the island-hopping saga of America in the Pacific war. The problem of finding a surfacing material for the airstrip is solved by dredging live coral from the reef and watering it with milk trucks to keep the coral insects alive and the landing field springy and porous. On this life-saving strip, Bus Adams, forced down in his shot-up SBD fighter plane, is the first to land—on the eve of the day

when the flight of bombers arrives just in time to begin operations against Kuralei. The builder is not there to greet them.
A crazed Jap, using himself as a living grenade, has committed
hara-kiri in order to destroy Commander Hoag, "a free man, a
man of thought and dignity, a man for whom other men would
die" (225). But above, the bombers wheel and come in for
their landings; from here they will proceed to Kuralei, to
Manila, and to Tokyo.

On the Konora airstrip, while waiting for the final giant
push against Kuralei, Bus Adams recalls melodramatic events in
the house of the Frenchman's daughters back at Luana Pori
on New Caledonia. The tragedy of the coming battle is made
more poignant by the remembrance of the soft arms of half-
caste Latouche Barzan and of her three beautiful sisters. This
plantation paradise, luxuriously furnished with pilfered American
comforts, keeps open house for all the American warriors.
Achille Barzan, Latouche's estranged husband, is hiding in the
hills from his own people; and Bus easily takes his place in her
bedroom. He forgets time and his wife back in the United States
until Tony Fry shows up; and then, with Bus an invalid after a
gallant fight with drunken Bill Harbison, Fry and Latouche
have an even more romantic affair. The unwanted husband,
Achille, is shot by Latouche in "self-defense" in a carefully
planned murder; and she and Tony are married in a Buddhist
temple ceremony.

At the end, all the sisters have done right by themselves.
Laurencin has married a Yankee colonel. "I wrote to my mother
about Laurencin," confides Colonel Haricot. "Her being half
Javanese, you know. Mom was very broadminded. Been giving
money to missions all her life." Josephine marries a sailor, who
had helped to win the beachhead at Konora. Marthe's sergeant
was not so lucky, but she was young yet and could look higher.
And, when Tony asks Bus to witness his will leaving everything
to Latouche De Becque Barzan Fry as his lawful wife, we fear
she too will find that her bruised heart can quickly heal.

The success of *Alligator* now depends upon a strike against
the fortified island of Kuralei. The last four sections of the
novel are all chapters in this operation, told by our narrator.
In "The Strike," he is assigned to the naval supply depot which
is the heart of the staging operation. In midsummer heat, this

area of two square miles of huts and dumps buzzes night and day with feverish activity. In command is Captain Samuel Kelley, a supply corps officer *par excellence*. Annapolis-trained and a strict disciplinarian, he arouses animosity and causes backbiting among his men; but the crucial work of preparing the fleet for the landing goes forward. What seem to be painfully unnecessary precautions by Kelley turn out to be vital when a hurricane strikes the supply huts; all goods have been stored in such a way as to support the walls against the destruction of the high winds.

The arrival of flyer Bus Adams to serve on the liaison staff arouses more animosity from Kelley than might be expected simply because Bus wears a baseball cap and refuses to defer to navy spit and polish. Tension mounts. An ammunition ship explodes in the bay before the eyes of four of the ship's officers who are drinking in the club ashore and who thereafter demonstrate that they are living on borrowed time. And one of them reveals the secret of Kelley's dislike of aviators. The incident is used skillfully by Bus to gain him a transfer to a fighting squadron. Next afternoon he is on his way north to share in the bombing of Kuralei.

In "Frisco" the narrator spends the night in an LCS off Kuralei during the first great Pacific bombardment. The fleet is in action all around them, and in the crew's recreation room the men get ready for the landing next day in which they will face the brunt of the Japanese shellfire. In their various ways, the men recall their last view of America and comment on the adventures of the cook and others with the girls of San Francisco, white and yellow. In one corner sits Norval, a twenty-three-year-old fireman. All during the grim night of bombardment, Norval sits in the corner with a file, honing his bayonet to a razor edge and sharpening his dagger and even the spikes of his baseball shoes. At dawn, "in the gray twilight of D-Day the first wave was going in. Fire raked them as they hit the coral. Jap guns roared in the gray dawn. Men, human beings on two feet, men, crawling on their bellies over coral, with minds and doubtful thoughts and terrible longings. . . . Men took over" (304).

"The Landing on Kuralei" is Michener's full-dress battle piece. The strategists had been outguessed by a clever Japanese officer who had fortified the promontory overlooking the two landing beaches to the south of the vital island fortress. After a bloody repulse at Red Beach and Green Beach, Admiral Kester is forced to put into action an alternative landing at what the men at once christen Sonova Beach. Tanks battle tanks, planes fight planes, shells from battlewagons fall on friend and foe. Amid the typhoon of lead, human beings crawl from trench to trench and after dark win the blockhouse with searing flamethrowers. The battle plan, at immense human cost, is on schedule after all.

Some of the men of the previous tales appear again. Those of LARU-8 are in a transport that suffers a direct hit. Dr. Benoway gets off with a wound in the leg. Bill Harbison, of course, had managed to get transferred back to the States four days earlier. And Tony Fry, beachmaster, although told to stay behind, rushes into battle to repel a surprise flank attack: "The Japs got him right away. Two slugs in the belly. He kept plugging along. Finally fell over" (316).

Fry and the rest had reached the end of the long line extending from safe civilian life in the States all the way out through Noumea and Guadalcanal and the landing craft to the storming of the blockhouse. "No matter where along that line you stood," realizes the narrator, "if you were not the man at the end of it, the ultimate man with his sweating hands upon the blockhouse, you didn't know what war was. . . . By the grace of God you would never know" (317). The battle drops to a lull as two buddies settle down for the night in their foxhole. The gist of their argument is: Was the landing as bad as they feared it would be? And would the other landings be even tougher? This section foreshadows the remaining years of World War II not described in this novel.

V *Men Lost in a Strange World*

After the crescendo of "The Landing on Kuralei" comes the diminuendo of the final chapter, "A Cemetery at Hoga Point." The narrator, with nerves shaken by the baptism at Kuralei, is on leave, fishing off Konora. Set ashore near the American cemetery on the cliff, where under the waving flag lie 281 dead heroes, he ponders the meaning of war and life. He chats with the philosophizing Negro caretaker, to whom the men in the graves are friends. The best-tended grave is that of Commander Hoag, "about de bes' man I met in all de Navy," for to him colored men and Jews and Italians were equally human and fine.

At Hoga Point there are no officers and enlisted men; there are only *men*. Here is the grave of First Lieutenant Joe Cable, USMCR: "He go after dem Japs plenty tough. . . . Finally he git his. Go down all in a lump. Dey tell me de colonel see him go. . . . I figger he pretty glad he let de lieutenant outen de brig. But maybe he ain' so glad, neither. 'Cause if he keep de young man locked up, he be alive now" (324-25). Liat's lover is merely one of the heroes at Hoga Point, about whom the care-taker—back home in Mississippi he used to call himself a "preacher"—can continue to speculate. For "Each man who lay on Hoga Point bore with him to his grave some promise for a free America. Now they were gone. Who would take their places?" (325).

Of his final chapter, Michener himself has commented: "Most perceptive readers of the book felt that the last story, 'A Cemetery at Hoga Point,' was the best thing in it, an opinion with which I am somewhat inclined to agree, for if I had any purpose in writing it was to extol the brotherhood that we seem able to attain only in cemeteries."[10] We know that he usually does have a purpose in his writing, and we can guess that the main theme of the book does have much to do with the idea that all men are brothers under the skin, and that the crucible of war hastens the process of revelation of character.

Awakening did come to many Americans during the tests of the Pacific war. They found they could be brave or cowardly; enduring or despairing; and, above all, blind to or able to see the common humanity beneath uniforms or dusky skins. The attitude toward interracial love evident in such stories as "Fo' Dolla'," "Our Heroine," or "Those Who Fraternize" was responsible for Michener's main expression of opinion when the musical play *South Pacific* came to be staged—in fact, his only expression.

"I had absolutely nothing to do with the Rodgers and Hammerstein musical and did not even attend any of the rehearsals, seeing the show for the first time in the final run-through," he said in 1956.[11] "I contributed no dialog, no additional story line, no staging ideas."

. . . I recall that after the tryout in New Haven, a group of experienced theatrical people who wanted the play to be a success visited me to see if I could persuade Rodgers and Hammerstein to remove from the second act their song on race relations, "You Have to be Taught." Many others brought heavy pressure on them to eliminate this controversial number, but the authors replied sturdily that this one represented why they had wanted to do this play, and that even if it meant the failure of the production it was going to stay in. And as the well-wishers foresaw, many of the major reviews panned the song, as an interruption. But as the play matured it was found that this song was more often praised than any other. I think that courage and determination such as this count for something in art.

The play was banned in South Africa in 1964 as "a plea for the mixing of races."

The themes of the novel are made flesh in a wide variety of characters who under the stress of war in the tropics reveal themselves as brave or craven, broad-minded or prejudiced, passionate or cold. Michener gives a broader view of men and women in the Pacific, at play or on operations, than any other novelist of World War II. They are shown on PT boats, on landing craft, on battleships, on ammunition carriers, and on submarines; they are men of the Supply Corps or the SeaBees or repair units; they are doctors and nurses; they are cacao planters or coast-watchers or Australian missionaries; they sit on lonely atolls or dash ashore in combat to die. Of special interest are men like Tony Fry, who says: "I like these islands. I've got some cash. Maybe life here is what I've been looking for. This Pacific will be the center of the new world. This is our future. Well, I'm part of it. This is for me" (276). Have other Tony Frys returned to the Pacific after the war to settle an American frontier in this ocean?

The action of the novel is varied as well. Plots of the different episodes range from almost nothing ("Alligator") to complicated melodrama ("Those Who Fraternize"). Although the novel culminates in combat, many chapters deal with other types of conflict.

Perhaps the most enduring value of *Tales of the South Pacific* is the use of setting. Michener's first-hand knowledge of almost all his scenes and his deep understanding of the history of the region enable him to utilize local color as a motivating force in the evolution of character.

Dealing with the earlier years of the war, when all the native glamor and jungle riot had not been leveled by the bulldozers, Michener was freer to depict the effect of the environment on Americans. He reveals also that he is aware of the provincialism both of the natives and of the Americans; and he uses it for plot purposes. Preoccupation with the exotic might open him to the charge of being a naïve romanticist. However, his reportorial eye was so keen that through it we see the Pacific with a wealth of sharp detail. He can spend three paragraphs to describe a sunrise (183) or to render a hurricane (293). He can stop to depict with realistic care the colors of a cacao grove (102) or the horrors of a land-crab invasion (228, 234). He mentions that the men in the southern hemisphere see Orion upside down. Other men in a quonset hut on the morning of a hot day can hear the metal "expanding in little crackles. New men always thought it was rain, but it was the sun" (57). He can explode our preconceptions by the casual remark that Segi Point is "the only place out here I know that looks like the South Pacific" (80). Realistic treatment of exotic materials by a writer such as Michener is not mere dreamy romanticism.

Michener was surprised and pleased that his novel was selected for a Pulitzer prize; for, as he said, "if I held no great brief for the stories as art, I was indelibly convinced that they could never be challenged as a truthful and sometimes probing analysis of men lost in a strange world."[12] He had hopes, too, that his volume would be a "solid emotional source book of the Pacific," particularly for future work by unknown authors. "Some very great novels are going to come out of the Pacific experience," he predicted in 1948.[13] In that year appeared Norman Mailer's *The Naked and the Dead,* and thereafter such Pacific war novels as James Jones's *From Here to Eternity* and Ira Wolfert's twice-written *An Act of Love.* But in 1951 Michener stated that he thought the great novel of the Pacific war was still to be written.[14] Quite likely, *Tales of the South Pacific* is that book. Looking back, we feel that the best picture of what that war was like is to be found on Michener's broad canvas. Who has painted a better one?

CHAPTER 3

Homeward Journey and Return

MICHENER, SPEAKING in 1948 to some students at Washington and Lee University, was angered when one of them remarked: "It's easy for you to write. You've traveled." He responded that it was his intention never again to write about foreign lands. "The writer's job," he added, "is to dig down where he is. He must write about the solid, simple things of his own land."[1]

Michener was working at the time on a big book tentatively titled "The Homeward Journey" and published early in 1949 as *The Fires of Spring*. It was truly about solid, simple American things. More than slightly autobiographical, it was the sort of book about growing up in the world that most writers turn out as a first novel. Unconventional as usual, Michener wrote his "first" novel second.

As a free-lance writer, Michener could have continued for several years to sell stories in the vein of his Pacific fiction. "Yancey and the Blue Fish" might easily have appeared in *Tales of the South Pacific*—it appeared in the *Ladies' Home Journal*. It concerns a tattooed Georgian, a "mustang" officer risen from the naval ranks, who fights the war with vigor even though his worthless wife back home has run away and deserted their daughter. Yancy, helping to occupy the island of Emirau which flanked the Japanese bases at Kavieng, specializes in rescuing and resettling island people who have suffered under the Japanese. He is a leader in the establishing of a new village on the island of Mussau because he speaks Chinese, and it seems for a while that he is able to sublimate his love-life only by his almost lunatic efforts to keep alive a transparent blue fish picked up on the reef. When he hears that his wife has returned home,

Yancy forsakes the lovely Chinese refugee girl and tosses his fish bowl over the cliff.

Another *Journal* story, which could have been written by others familiar with the campus setting during the overcrowded post-war conditions under the earliest G.I. Bill, is "The Empty Room." The self-pitying dreams of a mourning faculty couple who lost a son in the war are broken by the demand that they house two young veterans. The complications are slick but plausible, and at times the sincerity of the theme overcomes the soapiness of the plot. The women's magazines lost nothing when Michener decided not to spend time writing short stories that others could do as well as he.

Only one other uncollected story appeared in this period: "Out to Pasture," published in *Nation's Business* in 1949. It grappled with the plight of the man who comes up to retirement age without being prepared to replace his office career with anything else. Michener's answer to the problem seems to be that it would be merciful to let the poor fellow keep on working only as long as he might take to adjust to leisure.

I "People, Just as They Are"

The Fires of Spring, like these three stories, was written before Michener's share in the Rodgers and Hammerstein musical play gave him an assured income. The book is indeed about Americans in America; and, although David's travels cover a number of states, it centers around his boyhood in Doylestown, Bucks County, Pennsylvania; his summers as a cashier in an amusement park near Philadelphia; his college career at an institution not too different from Swarthmore; his travels on the Chautauqua circuit; and his struggles in Greenwich Village to learn the craft of the writer.

David is deliberately a less interesting character than the people he encounters. Michener was aware, however, of the danger of portraying a pallid hero. And David is more than an average lad; few young Americans of his time were orphans living in a poorhouse, or self-supporting short-change artists at the age of fifteen, or traveling actors or protégés of rich bootleggers.

Nonetheless, thousands of young Americans have found in

this book frankness and a voicing of their own attitudes, to which they respond gratefully. Of *The Fires of Spring* the author has said: "I get more mail about it than about anything else I've ever written, and a good deal of the mail is almost illiterate. It has a tremendous appeal for young people, particularly for boys in military service or people away from home for the first time. . . . I am somewhat depressed by the fact that the IQ of the people who praise it to the skies, judging from their handwriting, would not be very high."[2] This book was also the Michener title most immediately recollected as enjoyable by John F. Kennedy.[3]

Critics who expected another *Tales of the South Pacific* were less enthusiastic than Michener's correspondents about *The Fires of Spring*. Orville Prescott reported: "Mr. Michener is fine with his host of minor characters. But the passionate women in David's life are less convincing, and David himself is of little interest. *The Fires of Spring* is somewhat sentimental and sententious."[4] A similar basic weakness in the lack of definition of David's character was noted by G. D. MacDonald, who added: "The first two sections with a poorhouse and amusement park background are brilliantly done."[5] William Du Bois agreed that "For all his haste, Mr. Michener's anger at life is sincere. It is a pity he did not let his notes age a bit longer—or, at least, that he did not take the time to dramatize his anger in believable terms."[6] Perhaps the fairest review was that of Horace Reynolds, who said, in part: "There are commendable things in this novel. Mr. Michener writes with gusto and a good sense of story. . . . The stream of American life through which the hero walks, seeking both its meaning and knowledge of himself, is well realized. . . . Mr. Michener is addicted to melodrama, violence, and coincidence, and his story does not have the clarity of outline, the control and reserve his character David finds in Henry James."[7]

In Part I, "The Poorhouse," David Harper, eleven-year-old orphan, is living with his aunt, Reba Stücke, in the county home. She beats him often, but the old inmates are usually kind to the boy; and the home is an exciting place where an alert, sandy-haired, freckled kid can observe life. Like Huck Finn, David is exposed to tragedy and violence. He twice discovers old men who have hanged themselves; a homosexual is found floating in the water tank; David wrestles with a madman, Luther; and he watches a mad woman eat flies. He has early experience of the paradoxes of sex—his friend Toothless Tom is caught peering at little girls on the bank of the swimming hole. David feels a fondness for Marcia Paxton, a Quaker girl, and with borrowed pennies treats her and her family to loganberry juice at Paradise Park.

Most of the year, David finds life satisfying. But "Spring in a country poorhouse is a time of pain. . . . The men do not await refreshing breezes. They await the haunting memories of their youth" (21). In David, cheerful failures like Old Daniel see a promise of fulfillment that is worth all their encouragement. The boy's desire to write springs from his disillusion when he discovers that Hector and the other heroes of Troy could be beaten. "When I write a story," he explains, "the good people always win." Old Daniel forbears to deal the blow that would make the lad face too early the grim inexplicability of things as they are. Yet on his deathbed, Daniel does try to advise David and to explain to him that the earth is not an evil place: "But it's quite possible for a man in America to lead a good life and die in the poorhouse" (38).

In this limbo, roles are reversed. David is a child, but he is getting an education. "He was the man! He was the man who would avoid the terrible errors that had brought them to the poorhouse. And they were the children, looking forward to the distant day that would never dawn for them" (8).

Part II, "Paradise," shows David leading a double life. He is a ready learner in high school, especially when Miss Chaloner opens to him the magic door of mathematics; and he is also a star forward on the basketball team. In the summers, he is a skilled cashier at Paradise Park, who has learned not to cheat unduly the company that hires him but who is an expert at short-changing the yokels by all the arts of coins or bills. He resists the temptations of the little crook Max Volo and the pessimism of hard-hearted Mr. Stone, to whom "people are cattle." He is a friend of Captain John Philip Sousa, of the bandmaster's singer Mary (later Mona) Meigs, and of the sensitive European musician Klementi Kol, who initiates David into art galleries and to the candors of Hardy, Balzac, and Oscar Wilde.

David still lives in the poorhouse; but, when working at Paradise, he is a man of the world. And at fifteen he falls in love with an unattractive little prostitute who lives in a den under the Coal Mine concession. He pays her way to spend the winter in Colorado to help her lung condition, but she goes off with a man to Florida instead. When she returns, he makes an assignation with her that would have been dangerous to his future. This human bondage is ended an hour before the meeting when Nora burns to death in an accidental fire. David does not play the Dutch bundling game enjoyed by his schoolmates like Harry Moomaugh. But Marcia Paxton's lips are cool, and Mary Meigs does not object too much when his boyish kiss musses her coiffure.

Recipient of a scholarship from a mysterious donor—in Part III, "Fair Dedham"—David enters Dedham College as a freshman. He goes through a busy period of further intellectual and emotional awakening. What seems to the reader like one year is really four years. At this Quaker college, which bears some resemblance to Swarthmore, David falls under the spell of the White Russian mathematics professor, Tschilczynski; but he finds that there is "no mathematical certainty in life" and that the professor does not have all the answers. Nor does David's pal Joe Vaux, the radical Bostonian Irishman. Iconoclastic young Mr. Thorpe broadens David's appreciation of modern art by disburbing his old convictions. But not even Doc Chisholm, who teaches David how to read a novel and to enjoy cowboy songs, can remain the true messiah, even though he points out that books are the spirit of man and "the spirit of man jes' plain ain't purty. Yew can call it magnificent or bewilderin' or powerful to the point of despair. But it ain't college-English purty. And yew ought to stop writin' as if it was" (237-38). David concludes not to be a mathematician but to study people: "'People, just as they are.' And that was the beginning of his education" (238).

II *Chautauqua and Greenwich Village*

David's progress as a scholar is disturbed by his affair with Mona Meigs, now a lovely vaudeville actress. She is the mistress of kind Kol Klementi, but she satisfies herself with the passion of young David when Uncle Klim is away on concert tours.

When David and Mona are caught at last, they gaily go to a college "prom"; Kol, with his last illusion gone, shoots himself. When Mona decides to storm Hollywood, she gets David to borrow five thousand dollars from Max Volo, now a big-shot gangster. David's involvement with Max and the bacchanalian rout almost causes him to fail on his Chaucer paper, but he fights through his week of honors examinations and is awarded a *summa cum laude* amid cheers from "the only American college where the student body could get as excited about distinguished scholarship as it did about football" (266).

David is awarded a fellowship at the University of Chicago, and he starts to spend the intervening summer working on the Paxton farm near New Hope, with echoes of great poetry running through his head. It is clear that he and Marcia will soon marry and settle down, but David is not yet ready. He has not seen anything of his native land, broad America. "He did not want to be a college professor. He felt that surely somewhere there must be a more urgent life than that. Nor did he want to marry Marcia." When a phone call comes from Mona, David is ready to say farewell to Doylestown and to hit the road.

In Part IV, "Chautauqua," it is the summer of 1929 and the end of an economic era. It is also time for the last appearance of the traveling tent shows of the Chautauqua circuit. Mona has recommended David to be a low-paid juvenile actor, puppeteer's assistant, and general roustabout in the Cyril Hargreaves Troupe of Broadway Players. She is the ingenue and the mistress of sixty-six-year-old Director Hargreaves, who takes the role of Judge Hardy in *Skidding* and saves on cast salaries by handling a dozen other roles on the stage telephone.

If, as Michener suggests, growing up is the process of seeing things as they actually are, then the knowledge David gains from his fellow members of the troupe brings greater maturity. He admires dwarf Vito Bellotti, who plays the boy Andy Hardy and manipulates the strings of the puppet show while scanning the audience for a girl dwarf that he might be able to marry. David also admires the frank hedonism and love-making of Wild Man Jensen, ex-football star and truck driver. Most of all, he learns about life and the glamor of the stage from Emma Clews, for some reason called the Gonoph; aged forty-four and a dumpy theatrical veteran, she attaches herself to David and helps him see things as they are.

David rubs against the beauty, the harshness, and the mystery of America during the summer tour. He also begins to see life not through the eyes of others but through his own. The terrifying tornado episode tests his courage and reveals the truth that the world is "a superb flowing organization of people of which he was not the selfish center. Whether he lived or died was of no moment; and that discovery—which many young men never make—was the threshold by which David passed from callow youth to manhood" (317). But even when vengeful Hargreaves lies to Max Volo and gets David beaten up by the bootlegger's henchmen, the young man holds no grudge. He is learning that the motives of people are seldom unmixed strains of good or evil. And his jealousy of Jensen's acting ability strangely leads David to find a bride for Vito, the dwarf.

In Part Five, "The Valley," threads of lives are re-entwined and at last unraveled. In the winter of 1931 David has come to Greenwich Village—"the hidden valley between the breasts of Manhattan"—to learn how to be a writer. Through Alison Webster, a pretty young redhead he had met during his Chautauqua days, he gets a job with Clay Publications, which turns out more than a score of pulp magazines—the "cleanest filth" purveyed to the mass of America's literates. He works for the gifted Morris Binder, born editor and armchair detective who loves music (he has rigged up, with half a dozen radios, a set foreshadowing the hi-fi of today) but who cannot attend concerts because he is subject to unexpected convulsive fits.

Alison writes for money and knows all the clever tricks, but David hates himself when he yields to the temptation to turn out anything insincere. She is on the way up but he is content to live in the bohemian boardinghouse of Mom Beckett on MacDougal Street, just off Washington Square with its ghosts of Eugene O'Neill and Theodore Dreiser. Mom, a battling Amazon from Arizona, doesn't write books; she "lives them." In her lifetime she has fed more than forty writers as if they were stray animals; David, along with the rest, is termed a "horse's ass" for thus wasting his effort. Mom supports Claude, a bearded innocent who is "America's greatest poet," and pays for the publication of his verses; but she also makes him put together the meals whenever she has fired the Chinese cook.

After a year as assistant editor for Clay Publications, David is forced to join the jobseekers of March, 1932. There is no place for him in the depths of the depression, and he sweeps out the boardinghouse and lives on Mom's handouts, shared with Mona Meigs, who is again broke. She has deserted the dying old Hargreaves; David helps her and even the old actor. For a while he is happy with Mona, until she goes off to become Max Volo's "moll."

The next winter Reba Stücke dies, but her savings are tied up and David has to borrow fifty dollars to bury his mother's sister. In Bucks County he finds that Marcia Paxton, who had married Harry Moomaugh, is hurting the family name by getting a divorce. Mona Meigs dramatically returns to David to hide out from the gang murderers of Volo but then obtains publicity by putting "the finger" on the culprits. When her next "big chance" arrives, David submits to the abasement of masquerading as her chauffeur. He becomes encompassed in the vast ugliness of human life in a violent world. Yet it is the same world in which Max Volo secretly donated the cost of a fine young man's college education.

David, writing his novel at last and saving his pennies, lands in the hospital; and there he finds Marcia doing penance in the wards. When Miss Adams, Binder's secretary, nurse, and mistress, murders her boss because he is losing his mind, jobless David is thrust into the editor's chair. But he quits that post to go back to Mom's, finish his novel, and return to Bucks County. Ironically, his aunt's savings are given to Mona Meigs for another "big chance"—the Harpers do not wish to start their married life with poorhouse money. Journeying homeward, after a humble Quaker wedding, David and Marcia have found themselves at last.

III *Cleansed of the Autobiographical Itch*

Since *The Fires of Spring* is primarily the portrait of a literary artist as a young man, we expect and receive a number of comments about writers and writing. For instance, Doc Chisholm recommends to David the reading of "mordant novels"

—those which cut away all pretense from the inner being of the reader. "Mordant novels are often ugly novels," he says. "There is sand and gristle in them, and Ah can't name four that are well written." He directs his students to *Moby Dick, Casuals of the Sea, Oblomov,* and *The Old Wives' Tale.* It is more than probable that Michener feels the best books are those which have not only strong themes but high intensity and impact on their audience.

The financial contrast between great writers such as Claude and a cheap hoodlum standing in the bar with a roll of greenbacks is also ironic. In this world, writing as an art has nothing to do with marketable writing such as manufactured by David for *Bare Confessions, Real Love,* and *Rodeo Yarns.* And Claude gives David the best distinction he has heard between a novel and a poem: "A novel is a golden kettle into which you pour all of experience. . . . A poet tries to say it all in a few lines." Good poems are "distillations of books" (398).

In a moment of dedication, David realizes: "Writing is like that. Seeing what no one has ever seen before and writing it down so simply that everyone will say, 'Of course! I knew that all along.' If I can see, I can write. . . . If I could see into the core of some one thing each day, say a horse eating oats, or a ferryboat, or the way a chair stands on the floor, I'd soon be so terribly filled with material that they couldn't stop me from writing. Not even with machine guns. . . . There's no reason why I couldn't write as well as Balzac" (420).

David creates whole chapters of the novel in his mind, feeling almost as good as if he had committed them to paper. The characters, still nameless, come to have greater reality for him than people he meets on the street. Once he spends a whole day trying to evolve a name for a woman. He conceives the idea that, if he could only find the right name, his book would be half written. Like a pregnant woman, he feels embarrassed to talk about the ideas he is carrying. He feels that too much talk might bring his offspring bad luck (452). Later he begins to experience

one of the most unbelievable phenomena of art. He had a novel completely written in his mind. . . . Yet he could not write!
How can it be that a man can even see the finished printed

page in his eye, can taste the plaudits of a job well done, and yet be unable to push a pen across a paper or strike one reluctant key? . . . He had never previously bothered about drinking, but now when he could borrow money from Mom he wandered into one recently opened bar after another, explaining to anyone who would listen the details of his book.

(465)

David gets most encouragement from gray, prim Miss Adams, the secretary of Clay Publications. She predicts he will be a fine writer, but she heavily edits his opening paragraph by knocking out words. He uses too many adjectives and adverbs, she says. "And David, please don't use words like *beloved*. If your little boy loves the barges, let him show it." But he objects strongly: "When I write I want everything that happens to be absolutely clear. If I think the reader won't catch it, I'm going to say it right out" (454).

Quite likely, the mature Michener would still be on David's side. Pope's maxim of "Be thou clear" appeals to him. Michener is less fearful of adjectives and adverbs than most American writers today. If he thinks that something is interesting or beautiful, he says so. For him, style is not the art of getting along without adjectives.

Did Michener try to pour into this "golden kettle," *The Fires of Spring*, more than the novel form can comfortably contain? The theme is strong, and is reinforced by many little homilies on life and love and education that caused reviewers to label the book "sentencious."

The characters are numerous, and each bears almost an allegorical position in the progress of the young pilgrim in search of himself. There is pattern in their appearance—David's bondage to Nora is repeated in his enslavement to Mona, who turns out to be the heroine of his novel manuscript. Mona is in many ways supposed to be much like David, but she has sold herself from the start to the Bitch Goddess. Some of the characters stick in the memory—the aging actor Hargreaves, the pathetic Gonoph, Wild Man Jensen with his signal broom above the back of the truck. Other characters, however, seem to have been devised for plot purposes or drawn from the stock shelf. Again and again, the autobiographical urge is evident in David's responses, and his life, like that of some of the other characters, is too close to actuality to enable the novelist to handle it with suitable "distance."

The plot is also a bit too pat. The path of David as a lad who strives to grow up has often been trodden before. The arm of coincidence—for example, in the timing of the death of Nora or the murder of Binder—is sometimes stretched to the fracture point. The final wedding scene is almost a curtain call for the cast.

Primarily, this novel is memorable for the use of setting observed by the author as he lived through his own growing-up period. Michener never was editor of pulp magazines, but it is possible for him to have seen and done most of the other things that David Harper sees and does. The college period and the Greenwich Village days have been handled better by other novelists. Most memorable of all are probably the early poor-house scenes and the warm re-creation of life while traveling the roads of America with the brown tents of Chautauqua.

In this early novel, which still seems too uncontrolled to have been written by the author of *Tales of the South Pacific*, Michener—like Thomas Wolfe—looked homeward and used up the material which his early life had accumulated for him. *The Fires of Spring* is better than most *Bildungsromane*. Its greatest value, though, is that it purged its author of the autobiographical itch. Thenceforward, as a born reporter, he would gather and reproduce the lives of many people less close to him, and he would also achieve again and again what Keats called "negative capability." Villages either in Pennsylvania or Manhattan could not continue to engage the man who had roved through Europe and the Pacific.

IV *Kim Sing Gets the Baby*

The Pacific, in fact, still beckoned to Michener. Royalties from the musical *South Pacific* gave him a steady income and freedom to experiment as an author. Despite his vow never again to write about foreign lands, he accepted magazine commissions to revisit and to report on the scenes of his first novel. *Return to Paradise* is in part the book of a former serviceman who comes back to his wartime haunts after a lapse of five years.

(Originally meaning Hawaii, the "Paradise of the Pacific," the term "Paradise" came to be extended to the whole Pacific region.)

This adventure, Michener felt, would be "intellectually honorable" if he tried to put his material into a form that had never before been used. He wrote a series of fact-crammed essays about all these places. Then he wrote a series of stories growing out of the themes of the essays. Thus the reader could see from each essay what Michener thought about the region, and from the companion story the reader could determine what the region thought about itself. This sandwich system of producing a volume that could not be wholly labeled either as fiction or as non-fiction was viewed with disfavor by everyone else connected with the enterprise; but Michener felt that for this particular purpose the device would justify itself. The format was paid the compliment of imitation by Eugene Burdick in 1961 in *The Blue of Capricorn.*

The resulting volume, avowedly a *tour de force,* was highly successful and was chosen as a 1951 Book-of-the-Month. Michener was called "a Gunther with a dash or two of Dr. Kinsey" by Riley Hughes in the *Catholic World,*[8] but his work was termed by the Chicago Sunday *Tribune*[9] "a brilliant book and a worthy successor to *Tales of the South Pacific."* P. V. Farrell remarked: "Michener conveys the beauty and color of the islands, sensitively and perceptively. More than that, he carefully, imperceptibly, without grinding any axes, reaffirms the human dignity of even the most primitive savage and our responsibility to respect it. This is most welcome now, when the peoples of the world are suddenly being 'discovered' by Americans, variously as customers for creature comforts, decimal points in a Point IV program, birth control prospects, sandbags against Communism, or eventually, votes."[10] Robert Payne concluded: "It is when Mr. Michener describes his travels that he is most convincing, and the mature eye, selecting fragments of experience from the past and then setting them against the present, possesses a splendid power of evocation."[11]

Return to Paradise will be read with pleasure for years to come, and to one who knows anything about the Pacific Ocean area the descriptive sections will remain classic treatments. Michener was, moreover, fully aware of the tradition of South Sea fiction in which he was working.[12] "No writer need be ashamed of punishing his legs while trying to reach the footsteps of Conrad, Melville, Maugham, or James Norman Hall," he remarks in "The Mighty Ocean," the opening section.

His apprehension that his long journey around the Pacific might result in another heartbreaking trip of disillusion was not fulfilled. He had not lost his fascination with the atolls, the jungles, and the sprawling Australasian cities, nor his zest for making a travel essay into a clearly focused medium of illumination. Indeed, he deliberately made his non-fiction colorful and exotic, but he rigidly excluded from the stories the lush overwriting so common in the usual "South Sea stuff." He succeeded so well that, when films came to be made from several of these stories, the movie makers found that to feed their scenarios they had to purchase the rights not only to the fiction but to the companion factual essay as well!

In addition to the prologue and epilogue, the essay sections of *Return to Paradise* cover nine regions. Most of the pieces appeared in *Holiday* magazine with color illustrations. The guidebook information they contain is not too dated, but the scenes and peoples of the places visited are the most memorable parts.

A section on the first region, "The Atoll," has been reprinted in college rhetoric books as an example of inspired structural skill. It was written, Michener told me, out of the practical necessity to explain to the ordinary reader just how an atoll was built and what it was like to stand on one. It is followed by portraits of several "atoll men" he has known, white wanderers such as the writer Robert Dean Frisbie, for whose daughter's book Michener later found a publisher. "Much romantic nonsense has been written about the atolls," Michener concludes. ". . . A thousand wastrels have befouled the islands; a hundred sentimentalists have defamed them. But there still remains this fact: when the great seas pound upon the reef, when the stars shine down upon the lagoon, there is a mysterious, fragile something that no amount of misrepresentation can destroy."

Wartime memories helped Michener make vivid his return to such hallowed spots as Guadalcanal, Espíritu Santo, New Guinea, and Rabaul. His essays on Polynesia, Fiji, Australia, and New Zealand served well to prepare me for my own year in the South Pacific. The visitor to Fiji, for example, cannot but recognize— as he drives around the rutted roads of Viti Levu—the "mynah birds," the unsmiling Indian women in their rainbow saris, the scowling shopkeeping Indian men, the grave children of the race that has outbred the gay Fijians in their own islands. Motivated by his hymn of praise for the Huka Lodge of Alan Pye, high priest of New Zealand fly fishermen, we spent some wonderful days in the mysterious white cottage on the banks of the brawling Waikato River near the volcanoes of the North Island.

Readers of Michener who learn that a planet can cast over the still waters of the Pacific a glow almost as bright as a northern moon-path will seek, and find, their own star-paths. For years to come, the readers of *Return to Paradise* will be aroused to see for themselves the Pacific wonderlands that are now opening up more and more to visitors, even though the Tahiti that Michener revisited in 1950 is already as lost as the "New Cytherea" of the bare-breasted Polynesian nymphs that greeted the seamen of Bougainville's day.

The stories accompanying the travel essays, because they were admittedly written to voice a theme about a place, were assumed by reviewers to have been mechanically turned out to fit this need. Actually, some of the "local-color" fiction in this book belongs with Michener's best.

"Mr. Morgan," which furnished the scenario for the superb Gary Cooper film "Return to Paradise," was one of the two stories in the book that appeared first in magazine form. The narrator is a young native of the island of Matareva. The clash between the sanctimonious and lustful churchwardens of Pastor Cobbett and the war-weary Yank, Morgan, who merely seeks a refuge, can arouse the reader's fighting spirit. Worth pointing out, however, is the fact that Morgan is a "moral zero" and the pastor, his opponent, does stand for a doctrine even though at first it is tyrannically enforced. This is not the usual island love story, either; Morgan does not realize how much Maeva could have shown him until she is dead of tuberculosis. Nor does it end with an American marriage in the second generation. Harry Faber,[13] pilot of the World War II C-47 saved by a night landing in the Matareva lagoon, does return to his paradise; but, because he is a "bird of passages," he is driven off by Morgan in the role of irate parent. Morgan's daughter Turia weds a native lad when she is properly pregnant. After the ceremony, Morgan spends his time talking things over with another old man, the saintly Pastor Cobbett.

"Povenaaa's Daughter" also is one of Michener's best stories. It is an easygoing evocation of post-war Tahiti, when the Americans returned to the islands—in yachts. The seventeen-year-old heroine, Teuru of Raiatea, is ordered by whiskery, drunken Povenaaa to go along with the more experienced Hedi to Papeete to find a rich American. But, instead, Teuru's charms are showered on unworthy objects. First she brings home a young French poet, Victor, who insults Teuru by asking her to marry him. He goes back to France, and she goes back to Papeete. Next she brings home the small, old British sculptor Earl Weebles, who dies and is buried by the straits of Raiatea after having created great statues of the Polynesian people who set out from there on voyages of high discovery. Next Teuru, going to Papeete for the third time, fails to make a smug marriage as did Hedi, but she rehabilitates the gin-soaked beachcomber Johnny Roe. Povenaaa is pleased when at last she brings home to Raiatea an American—but this one has spent all his travelers' checks and Povenaaa still cannot buy that secondhand jeep on Bora Bora. When Teuru finally has an American baby on the way, Kim Sing, local Chinese vanilla planter, wins it on a cast of the dice; and Johnny goes back to America on a yacht. The ending is happy: Kim Sing gets the baby and the mother too, in a proper island marriage. And, of course, it turns out that, since all Polynesian first babies are given away to a friend, Teuru is not really skinny old Povenaaa's daughter after all.

This story is long because time must be allowed for Teuru to pass through her various involvements with men of four nationalities. Space is also required for the creation of the atmosphere of Papeete and Raiatea, regions that will never again be the same as they were right after World War II.

V *What He Learned in Paradise*

In Michener's essay on Fiji, his almost universal charity for the nationalities of the world clearly does not extend to the immigrant East Indians who had come to those islands and, by raising large families, had outnumbered the native Fijians. "Soon," Michener predicted in 1950, "they will outnumber all the other races combined, and it seems inevitable that Fiji must one day become a colony owned, populated, and governed by Indians."[14] His story "The Mynah Birds" likens the restive, revolutionary Indians to the greedy, quarrelsome Asian birds which have invaded many a peaceful Pacific island and driven out the native avifauna. But Ramcheck Billimoria, the Indian fanatic, is contrasted with the lovely Indian girl, Pata Cadi, whom he stabs because she has been going with an American airport engineer, Joe Harvey.

The story also gives occasion for Michener to contrast a British official, of the sort that has effectively administered overseas possessions for generations, with the brash American State Department representative Louis Richardson McGurn, one of the breed that must now take over such administration in many far-flung mandates. The irony lies in the fact that Sir Charles's family admires American things, but McGurn is trying so hard to be more British than the British that he even legally drops his last name because it has Boston Irish origins! McGurn, trying to hold civilization together, considers Joe Harvey to be the new American barbarian who will damage our nation in the eyes of the world, but at least Joe is a warm human being. McGurn may become human only if his British sweetheart can extract the stuffing from his shirt and get him to relax at a yangona party.

"The Story" is set on post-war Guadalcanal. The narrator, a writer, is besieged like all writers by people who want to collaborate with him by telling him a wonderful plot which he will write down, dress up, and sell for a fortune. Such a person is cadaverous Larcom, marked by many years of living in the tropics. Like Captain Handy in James Norman Hall's great story, "Occupation: Journalist," Larcom has a story to sell, and it is a mixture of trite romance and raw reminiscence from his patchwork past. The climax is supposed to come when an American Marine from Brooklyn, who had found a Solomon Island valley of gold and then lost it, flies in frenzy into a mountainside. As he burns to death, the valley shines in a golden glow.

The author rejects the offer to buy the story but during later encounters with Larcom it transpires that there actually was a Brooklyn American and a valley, not to mention a Jewish father seeking the body of his flyer son. It further develops that Larcom had played a heroic role as a coast-watcher on Bougainville, and that he had cherished a promising son, murdered by the Stern Gang in Jerusalem. The story of Larcom's life is more dramatic than any literature Larcom could fabricate. And again Michener's sympathies for men and women of all races is woven into the narrative.

Interracial tension is prominent in the Espíritu Santo story, "The Good Life." The narrator, a British civil servant of the Anglo-French Condominium ruling the New Hebrides, gingerly participates in the gay life of the French cacao planter, Perouse, whose home much resembles that of De Becque in "Our Heroine." Perouse likes to live at peace not only with his imported Australian or French girl guests but also with the Tonkinese laborers such as Nguyen Bo, whose family works hard to improve its lot. Perouse becomes unpopular by figuratively labeling as a "murderer" anyone who thinks he can keep backward races backward much longer. A riot on the eve of Bastille Day results in the literal murder of Nguyen Bo and his wife and in the maiming of Perouse. But Perouse survives to carry on his ideas of the "good life" through a slow evolutionary improvement and through the immediate adoption of Nguyen Bo's beautiful teen-age daughters. "The Good Life" is the only story in the book in which no American character appears.

The New Zealand essay is reinforced by a lengthy story, "Until They Sail," which was recently made into a film by a British company. It covers the lives of the members of a Christchurch family from the eve of World War II through V-J Day. Captain Harry Neville, his wife, and their five children form a unified group which is slowly broken down through the war years. The menfolk are killed or wounded on the far edges of the Empire; and, through the volunteer gallantry of its soldiery, New Zealand is left undefended before the Japanese threat.

Then the American legions arrive, and the four Neville girls become involved, one after another, with varied samples of Yank lovers. Anne, the eldest and most prim, has a baby by a handsome lieutenant, whose family after he dies in the war invites Anne and the child to live in Oklahoma City. The youngest, little Evelyn, grabs even at a horrid New Yorker G.I. named Max Murphy. Delia, who has married a ne'er-do-well New Zealander later captured in Malaya, spends most of her time staying with American officers and cheering them up "until they sail" for places like Tarawa and Okinawa. And widowed Barbara, whose husband had died in Egypt, finally joins the ten thousand New Zealand women who married Americans and gets herself a sensible major from Chicago. Again the twin ideas of undergoing wartime shake-ups in settled opinions and of avoiding racial and national prejudices are underlined in this tale from the home front in southernmost Polynesia.

However, as a companion piece to an excellent essay on Australia, Michener does not even attempt a local-color story with a setting on that continent-sized nation. "The Jungle" starts on a vessel in Sydney Harbor, but no effort is made to dramatize any section of Australia as "Until They Sail" dramatizes New Zealand. Instead, an Australian couple, Captain Alec McNair and his dumpy, subjugated, prematurely aged wife, who has the ridiculous name of Citronella, are contrasted with an American couple. The husband, a former PT boat skipper named John Millstor, is taking his wife with him on a sentimental pilgrimage back to Guadalcanal in McNair's trading vessel.

Millstor, who has been slowly dominated by his wife, has lost the virile mastery shown by McNair. In the sociological jungle that is modern marriage, John is the giant kauri pine of Malekula which has slowly been destroyed by the thousand aerial roots of the parasitic strangler fig, his wife. She cuckholds him with McNair almost before his eyes, and his shame is only ended when in a hurricane he sacrifices his now meaningless life in an attempt at he-man heroism. But are we supposed to accept the McNairs as having hacked a better pathway through the matrimonial jungle? This story is disturbing because the Pacific setting merely makes overt the action of the enemy—which this time is "the American wife, tall, straight, thin limbed, carefully beautiful."

Least satisfying of all the stories to me is "The Fossickers." Perhaps the spirit of New Guinea is too primitive, too nebulous for any civilized writer to encompass. At any rate, Michener merely assembles slowly a cast of four foreigners—an evil Australian adventurer, an unlovely English woman anthropologist, a Dutch ex-administrator, and an American cameraman—and takes them up the Sepik River and into a native village. Then the first three start for the distant hills with a girl (daughter of the anthropologist and the village chief) who will lend comfort to the Dutchman. We are supposed to anticipate their fates. But the ending is just a beginning.

In "What I Learned," his epilogue to *Return to Paradise*, Michener concludes that, whatever the South Pacific has been in the past, it will be most important in the future as the meeting ground between America and Asia: "It is the highway between Asia and America, and whether we wish it or not, from now on there will be immense traffic along that highway. . . . Asia must inevitably become more important to the United States than Europe." After spending a year re-exploring the South Pacific, Michener directed himself to a wide exploration of Asia.

CHAPTER 4

Around and About Asia

W HEN JOSEPH CONRAD was a boy in the middle of
Poland, he pointed to a map of darkest Belgian Congo and
said, "When I grow up I shall go *there.*" When Jim Michener
was a boy in Pennsylvania, he came upon an article on Central
Asia in the *National Geographic* magazine and made a similar
vow. The result of Michener's dream was that he has lived in
more Asian countries than probably any other American—or, for
that matter, any Asian. His next three books all dealt in different
ways with various parts of the same great continent. The titles
are *The Voice of Asia* (1951), *The Bridges at Toko-Ri* (1953),
and *Sayonara* (1954). A fourth book, *The Floating World* (1955),
a scholarly study of the art of the Japanese print, which required
two years of his working time, will be mentioned in a later
chapter.

I *Proconsuls, Rajahs, and Mem-sahibs*

Feeling that an understanding of Asia, a region more than
five times the size of the United States, was absolutely crucial
to Americans, Michener set off to talk to as many Asians as he
could. Of some one hundred and twenty interviewed, he reported in *The Voice of Asia* on fifty-three individuals or groups.
Some of the interviews lasted eight or ten hours. Michener did
not edit the thoughts which he chose for inclusion. A helpful
technique, after an hour or two of recording answers to simple
questions, was for the interviewer to say, "Perhaps you have some
questions you would like to ask me." Then the problems that
were really bothering the Asian would be reflected in the
questions he fired at the American.

Michener's method upon arriving in a new country was to
state to the newspaper reporters that he wanted to learn as

much as possible about it. He would then hole up in his hotel room and for three days write down his notes on the previous country. The local residents would become crazed by the sound of his typewriter and deduce that he was writing a dastardly exposé of their land without having talked to a single person. They would then insist on arranging for him a series of inter-views—ones he could never have obtained for himself—to give him a proper perspective.

"I talked with people of almost every conceivable calling," the author noted. "And I can say that this overwhelming exper-ience of friendship, understanding and brotherhood has left me changed. . . . They are yellow, many of them, but they are also individual human beings who can be approached by every single psychological avenue used to persuade Americans" (11).

The volume contains six vignettes from Japan, five from Korea, four from Formosa, four from Hong Kong, six from Singa-pore, four from Indonesia, three from Thailand, two from Indo-China (which then was still being painfully retained by France), three from Burma, thirteen from India, and three from Pakistan. At the end of each section, Michener appended his "observations" about what he thought Americans should know factually about that region. The book ends with a section on "America and Asia" which embodies the author's more general conclusions about the continent, and it suggests some main lines for the guidance of Americans while thinking about their future attitude toward the revolutions in Asia. These "rules" should be even more pertinent today, when a decline of United States power can be averted only through "intelligence, tolerance, and hard work."

The Voice of Asia was very well received. "Highly recom-mended as a thoroughly painless, thoroughly serious, study of current history," was the verdict of H. P. Linton.[1] Marcus Duffield reported that "Ninety per cent of the interviews and all of Michener's 'observations' reflect his intelligent way of searching for greater understanding of the mind of Asia."[2] Robert Trumbull concluded: "Michener, both as a straight repor-ter and in his analytical passages, succeeds in giving a picture of complex Asia today that is clear and accurate, on the whole."[3]

The political situations in the Asian countries have shifted during the years since 1951. Crises in lands such as Korea and

Pakistan have simmered down, and those in others such as India and Indo-China have simmered up. It would be highly desirable if men like Michener were sent every year or two to make reports on the countries of Asia for the benefit of their fellow Americans; indeed, in many later articles Michener did just that.

Not only the "observations" but such portraits as "The Proconsul" (General MacArthur, treated in a less than worshipful tone) and "The Man Without a Country" (Anthony Brooke, last of the white rajahs of Sarawak, whose final abdication statement Michener helped to write) may have historical value.

The lasting value of *The Voice of Asia* does not lie, though, in its political acumen. The sketched profiles will endure as long as we cherish portraits of real human beings of other cultures than ours. "The New Japanese Woman," "Boy-San," "The Hard Way," "The American," "The Buddhist Monk," "Three Rupees, Sahib," "The Hungry Old Man," and "The Grace of Asia" will well repay rereading. Especially heartwarming are the vignettes dealing with those favorite Michener subjects— racial conflict and outmarriage problems. On these topics one appreciates "Reasonable Doubts at a Strip Tease," "The Marginal Man" (the Eurasian), "The Schoolteacher," and "The Sheikh's Women." On the subject of India's reforms in the area of these topics, the first five articles under that country are devoted to the new woman and the attempt to shatter the caste system. Michener is also fond of quoting an interview on one side and then another on just the opposite side; both seem equally convincing. Panel pieces of this sort are "The Optimist" and "The Cynic."

An edge of satire is found in "The New Mem-sahibs," which the author terms "The most widely read single piece of writing I have done."[4] Because it showed how an ordinary American wife could set up housekeeping in Asia and immediately acquire the fatal arrogance that got the British kicked out of that continent, it has been distributed by American corporations to new employees.

II *Voluntary Men in Korea*

Michener's concern with Asia, where he served as news correspondent during the Korean War, extended also to the field of fiction. *The Bridges at Toko-Ri* burst upon the public complete in an edition of five million copies in *Life* magazine for July 6, 1953, followed three days later by publication of the hardbound book. Its creation was not so lightning-like. Actually, Michener had planned a novel on Korea two years before, but he "couldn't get it off the ground." Six months later, he worked on a version about the Marine Corps, but put it aside as being too trite in plot. He turned then to work on the novel that later became *Sayonara*; but in February, 1952, he wrote a complete outline of the Toko-Ri story. He laid it aside three times, and might not have completed it for two or three years. But some of the editors of *Life* came to him and asked for a novelette. He related the plot, and the piece was commissioned on the spot. "The story I told them that day wasn't changed by so much as a comma when I came to put it down," the author said later. "When I talked to them, the hard work had been done."[5]

To brief himself further on the operation of the jet-fighter planes, however, Michener spent eight days on an aircraft carrier. Three of the pilots he met there didn't return—family men with children. Undoubtedly the technology of the story and the character of Harry Brubaker were strengthened by this close research.

Both in magazine and hardbound form, the reception of *The Bridges at Toko-Ri* was friendly. Riley Hughes, who had considered *Return to Paradise* the work of a combination John Gunther and Dr. Kinsey, said: "Mr. Michener's book deserves to be read as a splendid tribute to what he calls 'the voluntary men,' the men 'on whom the world has always depended.'"[6] Quentin Reynolds said bluntly: "Anyone who can read this magnificent novel without being moved should run—not walk—to the nearest psychiatrist's couch."[7] James Kelly in the *Saturday Review* reported: "Mr. Michener turns in his best performance. Always an acute observer of human character, usually a serious-minded and formidably informed reporter, he has been less at home as a fictioneer. But *The Bridges at Toko-Ri*, a honed-down story of action, ideas, and civilization's responsibilities, moves forward with the inevitability of literature."[8]

Several reviewers thought that the descriptions of machines were better than those of men. "Sure, his pilots are good Americans and two-dimensional human beings, yet what they do and feel and say sounds too frequently more like the Voice of

America than fine art," said H. D. Webster.[9] "Mr. Michener has Kipling's dangerous gift of making engines live," said Robert Payne, and added, "Mr. Michener is not so fortunate with his human characters. . . . Is Brubaker iron or jelly? . . . In these last pages Mr. Michener nearly makes up for the early failure. . . . He has entered more compassionate depths than ever before."[10] Charles Poore concluded: "It has streaky faults of over-emphasis, but *The Bridges at Toko-Ri* will stand with the best of Michener's tales of the Pacific. His ability to breathe new life into familiar characters made from his familiar blend of pathos, homily, hilarity, engine grease and valor serves him well again."[11]

The novelette, only a hundred pages long, is divided into three sections: "Sea," "Land," and "Sky." It opens with an exciting episode concerning the aircraft carrier *Savo*, driving toward the deadly shore of Korea in order to take aboard return-ing bombers. One of them has been hit and has to ditch near the carrier. But the crew of the ship's helicopter go to the rescue. Mike Forney, Irishman from Chicago who wears a kelly-green stovepipe hat to give reassurance to downed pilots, takes the chopper to the spot and his buddy, Nestor Gamidge, drops into the icy water and hooks the flyer to the sling.

The survivor, almost frozen, is Harry Brubaker; a veteran of World War II, twenty-nine years old, and a successful Denver lawyer, he doesn't want to be fighting a war in Korea. Revived, he reports to Admiral George Tarrant, who tells him that Harry's wife and two small daughters have managed to get to Japan in time to share his forthcoming leave. And after that, the admiral knows, he must send his best men against the almost impregnable batteries surrounding the crucial four bridges across the canyon at the enemy center of Toko-Ri. Will the American flyers knock out those bridges and make the commissars finally decide to quit the war? Or has America become too indifferent to stick out the struggle and make the sacrifices? Will America have to make her last stand against the Russians on the banks of the Mississippi?

During the "Land" interlude in Japan, in "the greatest liberty port in the world," Brubaker's idyll with his family is quickly disrupted when he has to travel to Tokyo to get Mike and Nestor out of jail. The Irishman, fighting over his Japanese sweetheart, has caused a riot that demands Harry's time and money to settle; but he can do nothing less for the pair that hauled him out of the deadly sea. The admiral explains to Nancy Brubaker about the bridges, because she at least must have some conception of what the war is about, even though most Americans don't know or seem to care.

In the final panel of the story, Harry and "Cag"—commander of the air group, an Annapolis professional slated for high promotion—streak over Korea in their Banshee jets to photograph the approaches to Toko-Ri in preparation for the bombing mission. Two hundred Communist guns bombard Cag's plane as it enters the valley and runs the gantlet through the pinpointed course, resolutely clicking its camera shutters. Once again, miraculously unscathed, "Cag" makes a photo run before returning with Harry to the *Savo.*

The sight of the bridges recalls to Brubaker all the doubts that might cause him to request permission to stay safely on the ship next morning, when the big strike would take place. But he is the best of the admiral's flying team. He is on the spot in Korea: "Might as well do the job." He calms his fear of physical cowardice by standing close to the plane catapult without flinching when its eleven-ton steel piston flashes at his face.

The climax of the book comes when the pilots dress for the final mission and take off for the strike. Despite the snowstorm of flak they complete the destruction of the bridges at Toko-Ri. But while he is returning to the carrier, a random bullet in his engine brings Harry's Banshee down in the paddy fields. Even though Mike and Nestor come to his aid, there is no hope for the airmen in this mud, for they are surrounded by snipers and grenade throwers. Mike and Nester die first. Finally the sky is empty, and Harry Brubaker is "alone in a spot he had never intended to defend in a war he had not understood." Only in the last fraction of a second before his death does he understand. The admiral, who had looked on Harry as a surrogate for his own son, is left to marvel: "Why is America lucky enough to have such men? . . . Where did we get such men?"

What Harry understood in the last second of his life is the theme of this novelette—that all through history free men have had to fight the wrong war in the wrong place and that the bravest few cannot shift the burden of sacrifice to anyone else.

The "voluntary men," on whom finally civilization must depend, cannot say: "Hold back the enemy but make someone else do it." Their wives, like Nancy Brubaker, may say, "If the government dared to ask women like me, this stupid war would end tomorrow"; but the men must fight the war because victory is more important than family. As at the climax of *Tales of the South Pacific*, Michener points out that only a few men are ever the spear point at the end of a long line of defenders, and only these ultimate men can know what war really is.

Perhaps the role of Brubaker is too heroic to be highly convincing. Other characters in the novelette stand by themselves. Beer Barrel, gigantic Texas farmer who mounts the carrier's deck to wave down the planes with his paddles while making microsecond decisions on life and death, remains in the memory. Coming aboard lugging two golf bags weighted down with cans of beer, he is a disgrace to the uniform but the sole hope of returning pilots who fear a crash. As the admiral says: "He flies against his bridges every day." Beer Barrel has one kind of bravery that a navy must have.

Other brave men are those of the helicopter crew. And another is the air group captain, "Cag." He must be ready to take the highest responsibility of command. For a while, it seems that he will back away from what he knows is right. But after Brubaker's death, "Cag" talks back to the admiral: "I don't care any longer what kind of fitness report you turn in on me because this was a good mission." He is ready for responsibility now.

Michener's concern for human brotherhood is exemplified again in the scene in the private pool at the hotel, where two families, American and Japanese, introduce themselves and paddle about naked in the sulphur bath, conversing without enmity.

The best part of this book is probably the description of what it was like to live on a carrier and to fly a jet plane in war. "It was terrible and supreme to be there, whistling into the morning brilliance," Harry realizes as he flies on the photo mission toward the Communist bridges. Reading of such exultation, one forgets Michener's wry confession that each time he himself flies in a combat jet he becomes violently airsick.

The use of propeller planes to "windmill" the giant carrier and to keep it from crashing against the quay, burning out expensive engines in the process, brings a shudder to the taxpaying reader. Two pages of detail describing Brubaker as he dresses in his pilot's "poopy suit" for winter flying conclude with a simile: "Harry Brubaker, who was about to soar into space with a freedom no previous men in history had known, was loaded down with such intolerable burdens that at times he felt he must suffocate; just as many citizens of his world, faced with a chance at freedoms never before dreamed of, felt so oppressed by modern problems and requirements that they were sure they must collapse" (99-100). Even the chance, fatal bullet in the Banshee's turbine carries with it an image: "Like the society which had conceived the engine, the turbine was of such advanced construction that even trivial disruption of one fundamental part endangered the entire structure" (122-23).

Full utilization by moviemakers of the resources of the United States Navy, as well as an outstanding cast, resulted in a full-color version of *The Bridges at Toko-Ri* that was one of the finest films of 1955.

III *Madame Butterfly in Swingtime*

Meanwhile, Michener had published a novel about Japan, which had come to be his favorite foreign land. *Sayonara* is not only a love story about a modern-day Butterfly but also a love letter from the author to a country that had been his greatest enemy only a few years before. As Pearl Buck put it: "The book is, for me, this author's best work, and it can and should be read for any or all of several reasons: as a moving story, told in spare strong prose; as illuminating description, original and unusual, of a rarely beautiful country; as a powerful portrayal of Americans and Japanese as they must now live together upon Japanese soil. But deeper than this, if anyone cares to go deeper, is the authentic explanation of why, if we Americans do not change, we can never win in Asia."

Sayonara appeared early in 1954, after having run in three issues of *McCall's* magazine. Of it Bradford Smith wrote: "He artfully conveys a sense of the sensitiveness, the artistic quality of Japanese life."[12] John Metcalf labeled it "his most serious and accomplished writing yet."[13] Although Frank Gibney remarked that "There are only a few flashes in it of the sympathetic observer and the fine literary reporter that Michener has proved himself to be,"[14] Fanny Butcher concluded: "*Sayonara* is written with a sensitive feeling for beauty of materials and expressions and it has a quality rarely found in modern fiction—moral conviction."[15]

The story of *Sayonara* was such that it soon had several Hollywood studios going into court to argue that the film rights belonged to them. In the book, Major Lloyd "Ace" Gruver, twenty-eight-year-old son of a four-star general, has just shot down his sixth and seventh MiGs in Korea, and is sent to Japan to rest and recover. His father's friend General Webster has arranged a cushy job for him near the general's daughter Eileen, a Vassar graduate to whom Ace is more or less engaged.

A stuffy West Pointer, anti-civilian, anti-Japanese, Ace gets involved in helping Joe Kelly, a tough kid in his unit who wants to marry a Japanese girl. Ace realizes that any such involvement would ruin his own career; but he soon falls deeply in love with Hana-ogi, a tall, cool girl, the greatest dancer in Japan, who plays men's parts in the Takarazuka theater near the marines' dormitory where Ace lives. He learns that her peasant father, who sold her into the theater life, had been killed by an American bomb; and her brother had been executed as a war criminal for his behavior toward American prisoners. But the flyer's bold approach wins her, and they set up a little house by a canal in Osaka, near the home of the Kellys—for Joe has overcome all the red tape and found happiness with his wife Katsumi.

Breaking with Eileen and her battle-ax mother, Ace risks ruin to experience what some half a million American men have sought—the devotion of a Japanese sweetheart. "Did I love Hana-ogi because I was afraid of American women?" he asks himself (134). Again the spoiled, bossy, selfish coldness of these women alienates their men, just as it does in "The Jungle" story in *Return to Paradise*. "I almost cried with pain to think that something had happened in American life to drive men like Mike Bailey and me away from such delectable girls" (138). He decides that the dedication of Katsumi and Hana-ogi to their menfolk is deeper than anything Eileen could offer. Eileen certainly would never erase the irritations of the day by scrubbing her husband's back in a big Japanese tub.

The rhapsody of the little house by the canal cannot last. Ace is put under house arrest by General Webster; and, when his father arrives and slanders Hana-ogi, Ace strikes him. Ace remembers that his father once persuaded him not to give up his West Point career, so he is hardly touched by his father's dictum that "Strong men have the guts to marry the girls who grew up next door." He and Hana-ogi move into the tiny home of the Kellys, and here Ace learns more about the Japanese women: "They had to do a man's work, they had to bear cruel privations, yet they remained the most feminine women in the world" (146). Some of them, naturally, were far from perfect as wives; in fact, "they were exactly like the wives of America; some were gentle mothers, some were curtain dictators and some few were lucky charms who brought their men one good thing after another" (168).

Hana-ogi is one of the real charms, he feels, especially after he wanders with her through the Japanese countryside and understands the soil from which she came. She has taken the name of a celebrated actress, "the most renowned prostitute in the entire history of Japan" (140), whose life is a perennial subject for the color prints whose strange artistry Ace comes to appreciate.

Ace decides to marry Hana-ogi and destroy his future. Paradoxically, he discovers that the age-old story of Butterfly is quite wrong. "Always the yellow girl tried to seduce these clean-cut men away from their decent white sweethearts" (203). He pleads with the girl to marry him, and it is she who refuses.

The Kelly family is blasted by an army order requiring Joe, a prospective father, to return to America and to desert his legal wife. Rescued by their Japanese neighbors from an anti-American mob, Ace and Joe still face tragedy. Joe and Katsumi take the romantic Oriental way out, and die in a love pact—ironically, just one day before the cruel order is rescinded. Ace is not even able to say *sayonara* face to face with his lost sweetheart, who leaves with her theatrical troupe. He returns to America, to promotion, to a glittering future, and to Eileen. "And you, Japan," he says in farewell, "you crowded islands, you tragic land—*sayonara*, you enemy, you friend." But he lives in an age when soldiering is the only honorable profession, and "the only acceptable attitude toward strange lands and people of another color must be not love but fear" (243).

The theme of this novel is clearly that many an American has found a profound satisfaction in marriage with an Oriental wife to whom her husband's needs are supreme. But in a profession as rigid as the military, such a marriage is not possible; prejudice is still too strong.

Again Michener found difficulty in creating an entirely convincing main character, for Ace Gruver is unbelievably prejudiced at the opening and unbelievably converted at the end. Heroic, he sounds conceited, probably because of the first-person narration. He seems more a victim than a chooser, less an actor than a patient. Nor does Hana-ogi really come through to the western reader as an appealing, credible companion. Their love affair seems forced, like the early-blooming chrysanthemums given to Ace by the friendly flower vendor. Oddly, the most plausible characters are those sketched with strong dislike: despotic Mrs. General Webster, whose bigotry is embodied into army orders; or Lt. Col. Craford, Southern autocrat who brands Ace a "nigger lover." Again some of the supernumerary characters, inhabitants of a strange country, are given with typical Michener sensitiveness—an old peasant farming his tiny plot of land with his fingers, a highly educated Japanese museum curator and scholar, a henpecked husband who flings away all his yen into a sparkling pinball machine.

The setting of the novel makes much of the Japanese cities and byways, the little paper-walled houses of Osaka, the glamor of the Takarazuka girls during a performance of "Swing Butterfly," the peaceful shrines of Kyoto, the puppet theater revealing the celestial charm of ritual suicide. Michener's growing interest in Japanese prints, which was to result in his gathering of a notable collection and the publication of four books on the subject, is revealed in his remarks about the appeal of the old Hana-ogi drawings.[16]

The humor of culture clashes is shown in such scenes as the one in which Ace braves the terrors of the P.X. lingerie department to buy "weekies" for Katsumi, who desires to be as American as possible for her G.I. husband. And the question of how two lovers without a common language can communicate is feelingly sketched in several pages, making attractive the overuse of a few handy words and Hana-ogi's *l*-less pidgin. She can say, "Rots peopre nebber rub nobody," but it is better when she dances out the story and uses her genius of mimicry to reveal her love.

The popular appeal of *Sayonara*, at its lowest level, might simply be an answer to the question: "What's it like with an Oriental girl?" At the highest level, it is again a warm *exemplum* on Michener's perennial theme of universal equality, of love as the catalyst of interracial tranquillity. Less than two years after the publication of *Sayonara*, Michener himself married in Chicago a girl of Japanese ancestry.

CHAPTER 5

Once More the Mighty Ocean

THE PACIFIC, where Michener had first won his laurels, still beckoned. He returned to this region for the materials for two more books—*Rascals in Paradise* and the big novel *Hawaii.* The first of these was the only book Michener wrote in collaboration, and it happened that I was chosen to be the junior author.

Michener was an editor at Macmillan when the manuscript of *The Spell of the Pacific* arrived, a big anthology edited by Dr. Carl Stroven and myself. Michener was so enthusiastic about the project that he offered to write an introduction, and we were delighted to accept. Soon we met in Honolulu, and thereafter kept in touch with each other. On November 15, 1954, hearing that I was soon to leave for a year in Australia as a Fulbright senior research fellow, Michener wrote me, in part: "I would enjoy collaborating with you on a book to be called something like *Wild Men in Paradise.* It would consist of about eight long, accurate, provocative, and poetic biographical essays on some of the worthies of the Pacific. . . . We would certainly have maximum color as one criterion, but we would also want to cover those typical and inherently interesting men whose lives have a chance of evoking large speculative problems." He named ten prospective subjects.

Naturally, I accepted with great gusto and suggested more than a dozen other candidates for biography, and a month later sent along six more. The final selection of ten persons, from our omnibus list of several dozen, included only four from Michener's original proposal.

I *Two Authors, One Book*

Early in February, 1955, Michener and the Bennett Cerfs were in Hawaii. Sitting in bathing suits on Waikiki Beach in front of the Royal Hawaiian Hotel, Cerf, Michener, and I discussed our project as a possible Random House book; and we informally reached agreement on contract terms.

Rascals in Paradise was titled, it happens, before a line of the book had been written. Bennett Cerf picked up a word I used to describe some of our prospective biographees. Despite the joint efforts of the collaborators to find a better title—since several of our men were not rascally at all—the editors resisted all suggestions to change. The title was finally attached to the opening chapter, which appears as "Rascals in Paradise: The *Globe* Mutineers," but we still get comments that Captain Bligh and Will Mariner were really quite honorable fellows.

The day after the Waikiki pact, Michener sat down with me in his tidy, impersonal hotel room, and we selected ten characters about which chapters would be written. Of these, two turned out to be unsuitable and were later replaced. Our plans were made at this time to divide up the chapters for the purpose of writing the first drafts. I then embarked on a ship heading for Fiji, New Zealand, and Sydney; Michener took a plane on his way to spend some months in Afghanistan.

The ten characters were chosen with a view to maximum coverage over time and space in the world's biggest ocean. In addition to Sam Comstock (1802-24), murderous harpooner of the *Globe*, they comprised the French Marquis de Rays, chief monster of the New Ireland colonization frauds (1880); Coxinga, master pirate of all time (died 1662); Walter Murray Gibson (1822-88), the power behind the throne in the reign of King Kalakaua of Hawaii; Captain William Bligh, who was involved not only in the *Bounty* episode but in three other mutinies and in five major courts-martial (1754-1817); Doña Isabel Barreto, our only lady subject, wife of Don Alvaro de Mendaña and directress of the disastrous voyage of 1595; Captain Bully Hayes (1829-77), last of the great Pacific buccaneers; Louis Becke, Australian trader, adventurer, and author (1855-1913); Will Mariner, the boy chief of Tonga (1791-1853); and Edgar

Leeteg (1904-53), brawling bohemian of Tahiti whose paintings on black velvet created a South Sea legend.

The scene of their operations was not only the open ocean but land areas from Peru to the China coast and from Hawaii to New Zealand, including episodes in the Marquesas, Tahiti, Samoa, the Dutch East Indies, Tonga, the Solomons, and Formosa. End-paper maps and a thorough index revealed the broad scope of the book, and extensive bibliographic references revealed the obligations of scholarship in research areas where materials were often slight or unreliable. Intentionally, the differences among the characters were also great. The main basis for final choice was that they were all strong-willed, dramatic, and energetic. Only slowly did it dawn on us that they all had one thing more in common: they all had seemed to dream of setting up some sort of private kingdom on a Pacific isle, which has long been almost the standard romantic symbol of escapism. Taking this cue, Michener wrote his excellent introduction "To All Who Seek a Refuge," directed to the escapists of our own troubled time.

The book that finally resulted from our joint labors stayed on national best-seller lists for ten weeks and was favorably reviewed around the country as well as in the British Commonwealth. It was translated into six languages abroad. I shall refrain from making judgments on its value and instead quote those of others. Darwin Teilhet said in the *Saturday Review*: "Not since Sam Clemens and Robert Louis Stevenson closed up shop in the Pacific has a gallery been opened as richly and satisfyingly mounted as *Rascals in Paradise*. . . . Commodiously informed, rich in detail, wonderfully varied, and a joy to read. One finishes it with the feeling not of surfeit but of wanting yet more, please."[1] "Adventure, glory, danger, riches and relaxation under the tropical sun—it's an illusion not to be trusted, say our old Pacific hands," remarked John K. Hutchens, and went on: "Their warning having been dutifully given and duly received, how soon would you like to start?"[2]

Charles Poore reported: "What stands out, though, is the painstaking way Mr. Michener and Mr. Day have sifted the records, the testimony of highly impeachable witnesses and the cool truths of court reports to find out, so far as may be possible, what really happened, what animated their galleries of scoundrels in landscapes where prospects pleased and men were vile."[3] Said P. J. Searles: "All the stories are excellent, mostly lurid, filled with high adventure, bloodshed and brutality. Messrs. Michener and Day have selected a dozen of the most picturesque characters in almost four centuries and the writing does them justice."[4] John T. McCutcheon, Jr., said: "Professor Day, an authority on the literature of the Pacific, and Mr. Michener, who has helped to create it, have assembled a new series of tales of the South Pacific—all of them true, this time, but still with the intoxicating atmosphere which always seems to result from mixing Michener with the Pacific. . . . These are tales it will be hard to forget."[5]

According to Walter F. Morse, "It deserves a permanent home among the classics prepared and designed for armchair explorers."[6] Said William Hogan, "Michener and Day seem to be the most efficient collaborators since Nordhoff and Hall (or perhaps the Rodgers and Hammerstein of 'South Pacific'). They have produced a man-sized book."[7] Richard H. Dillon wrote in the *Library Journal*: "An excellent volume overall, and highly recommended. It is a splendid sampler of the curious, colorful characters, most of them escapists, who have peopled—and who still inhabit—the South Pacific."[8]

Although I here abjure any value judgments on *Rascals in Paradise*, this chapter does offer a chance to present Michener in the role of literary collaborator, and to discuss the method he followed in that role.

Many people wonder how it is possible for two authors to write one book between them. I had previously collaborated on three books with friends, and had found such teamwork to be congenial when the partners, widely different in experience and knowledge, were agreed on general aims. From the first, I looked forward with zest to the chance to work side by side with Michener.

Outside of playwright circles, true collaboration is quite rare. Of course, the sort of "as told to" writing, in which one person has a story to relate but employs the pen of a trained craftsman to tell it, is a common thing, whether or not the "ghost" gets credit on the title page. But a real sharing of the writing task is not common. It is difficult enough for an author to create a work that will satisfy himself, let alone satisfy a partner who has his own ideas of what words will be the best. The bark of friendship of even Mark Twain and Bret Harte splintered on the rock of attempted collaboration.

Yet the Pacific region has somehow been compatible with true collaboration. Charles Nordhoff and James Norman Hall, neighbors in Tahiti, turned out no less than eleven books jointly, including the celebrated *Bounty* trilogy and six other volumes with Pacific settings. Robert Louis Stevenson and his stepson, Lloyd Osbourne, wrote *The Wrecker* in collaboration. Louis Becke and his journalist friend Walter Jeffery did several novels together (including *The Mutineer,* which concerned Bligh, the *Bounty,* and Fletcher Christian). D. H. Lawrence wrote *The Boy in the Bush* with Mary Louisa Skinner. In recent years, William Lederer and Eugene Burdick produced *The Ugly American.*

In all these instances, so far as I can find out, and also in others such as the better-known collaboration of Joseph Conrad and Ford Madox Ford (Hueffer) on the novel *Romance,* one writer would do the first draft of a section and the other would revise it. This was true of our own manuscript. The first draft of each was done by a single person. It was then rewritten back and forth until both were satisfied. Sometimes, neither could be quite sure that any particular passage was entirely his own words.[8] However, the chapters on Leeteg the painter and Coxinga the pirate were the two in which my participation was very slight.

II   *Research on Rascality*

Several reviewers assumed that it was my task to supply the facts of research and Michener's to supply the style. Actually, it worked out that a good many pages of my original prose survived without a great deal of rewriting by Michener; and he, working in the Library of Congress and elsewhere, did much digging for historical facts.[10] The facts in the final version of our book, except for one minor slip,[11] have never been controverted. Our interpretations of character, of course, were our own.

The minor difficulties of collaborating from a distance are amusing in retrospect. In my leisure time in Sydney I was able to collect a mass of usable facts in the Mitchell Library, which is probably the most valuable collection of materials in the world on Pacific history. Michener passed through Australia in the fall of 1955 on his honeymoon, but we did not meet because by that time I was working in Melbourne and his route lay at the opposite end of the island continent, through the cattle stations of western Australia and the ports on the Indian Ocean.

In Australia I was able to draft five chapters to carry back to Honolulu, but we did not get together until mid-April, 1956, when Jim and Mari arrived by ship from the Orient. Thereafter until mid-June, with almost daily consultations and much mid-night writing and revising, seven chapters were put into nearly final form. I never worked harder in my life, but trying to keep up with Michener was wonderful sport.

Then Michener returned to Pennsylvania, where he did the first draft of the Coxinga chapter; in Honolulu I wrote the two remaining ones. Heavy use was made of air mail for the rest of the work of revision and seeing the book through the press. Our correspondence file is almost as lengthy as the manuscript of this 150,000-word volume.

Further difficulties of collaborating with a world traveler are suggested by this paragraph from a letter Michener wrote me on August 10, 1956: "I also want to advise you that I am leaving New York on September 5 for Japan, Indonesia, Thailand, Burma, Rome, and New York, returning sometime after the election. . . . This means that I'll be incommunicado during some of the heavy working hours, but proof sent to me in Rome for October 16 arrival could be worked on."

No disagreements occurred during all the enterprise that were not amicably settled on the spot. At one time, I urged that Michener use fewer quotations in the Coxinga story; at another, he and the editors at Random House asked me to rewrite the chapter on Doña Isabel Barreto because the tone, spare and sarcastic, was out of keeping with that in the rest of the book.

The pleasures of watching a master craftsman at work were great. For example, I handed him the first draft of the story of the *Globe* mutineers with some trepidation. For years I had wanted to put this yarn into shape, but the events were so complicated and so many characters were involved that a unified narrative seemed impossible. "The trouble," said Michener after he had read it, "is that the main villian, Comstock, is killed half-way through the story. But the reader will go along with you if you frankly state that the *Globe* mutiny was not a single drama but several, and then go on to tell the amazing sequels." No less than five rewritings of this chapter, back and forth between us, were necessary. But the result set a definite pitch and was chosen as the opener for the book. Moreover, before *Rascals in Paradise* was published, an abridgment of this gory chapter appeared in four installments in a Sunday magazine with a twelve million circulation; of it, one editor wrote: "Our 37 newspapers have shown more enthusiasm for this series than anything else *This Week* has published in recent years."

Concerning the idea of an introductory section, Michener wrote me on July 19, 1956: "I think it extremely important that we get a concise, handsomely written preface. A good many reviewers and casual bookbuyers are going to look at this for a statement of what our book is all about. I want to present them with a moving testament and one that will excite their interest. I also want to explain how the book ties into their lives." The culmination of this attractive preface was his story, which was reprinted in all editions of the *Reader's Digest*, about the man who in the summer of 1939 decided to hide out during the age of world wars; and, by a process of keen logic, he finally picked out as the safest spot the Pacific island of Guadalcanal.

"Avoid using a lot of unnecessary proper nouns," was a Michener dictum drawn from his editor days. "If we don't refer to a man or a place at least three times, let's not trouble the reader by using the name at all." He was also careful to avoid words that verged on the pejorative, words like "Asiatic," "Chinaman," "half-caste," or even "native."

Early in the game I suggested that, since some Pacific places have their names spelled in a dozen different ways, we stick slavishly to the form in the printed Index of the National Geographic Society's map of the Pacific. Amused at himself, Michener confessed in a letter to me of August 10, 1956: "I have vacillated on this point several times and came up with a silly compromise that followed the Geographic except where my personal preferences were concerned. This leads only to confusion and I abandon it."

Another reward of close co-operation comes from this warm paragraph, in a letter to me of August 6, 1956: "Your foresight in sending me the Ferrando translation at the same time that I was asking you for it is a fine example of why I have found our collaboration so pleasant."

On the financial side, Michener was generous. He had worked out the main plan of the book and convinced his publisher of its soundness. When the time came to discuss terms of division with me of royalties on the book, he insisted: "Fifty-fifty. I don't want to work with anyone who can't carry half the load, and I would refuse to work with anyone who carried half the load and didn't get half the money."

Much better known than I in the market place, Michener rejected an offer to sell the Doña Isabel story, which we had researched together, to a magazine under his name alone. "There is, I find," he wrote me on February 9, 1957, "a temptation to capitalize on my participation in this and to try to leave you out." (This actually happened when, unknown to Michener, several chapters ran in a magazine in Australia with his name as the sole by-line.) "As you well know, I will not be a partner to such deals and have made it very clear to everybody involved that I would not be. So, although I might have done this and then split the money with you under the table, I just thought I ought not to be involved with it in any way."

Michener wrote all but five words of Chapter 10, depicting Edgar Leeteg, the artist of Tahiti. To this lengthy study Michener applied his lifetime *expertise* in art criticism. It also created the need for clarification of the author's loyalties to his subject and his readers. After publication, Barney Davis of Honolulu, Leeteg's last sales agent, wrote a lengthy letter objecting strongly to the tone of the presentation of the man he had made celebrated as "the American Gauguin." Michener responded with an equally lengthy, friendly letter in which he said, in part:

> I have been through this several times with other subjects, Barney. People get very angry about not getting the complete puff-job from a writer and then they realize later that because he does *not* do puff-jobs, what he does write is accepted widely around the world and actually does more good in the long run. . . . A good honest story always achieves more of what a

subject hopes will be achieved than a second-rate article which merely praises the subject in round and meaningless terms. . . . I always write from the basis of having somebody who knows a lot more about it than I come along twenty years later to review my work. . . . I think that in the case of Leeteg what I have written will last for a long, long time. It is a true account, it is a friendly account, it is in a sense a loyal account of a man whom I knew and liked. . . . As it is, people will be reading about Leeteg long after I am dead and everybody who writes about him will have to go back to what I have written to get the starting point on the facts of this man's life. To have accomplished such a basic statement is a very good thing and I hope that the events of history will bear me out that I have accomplished just that.

This response to Davis is an excellent restatement of Michener's idea that a writer who is insincere will not be read. Once he said to me: "I have been kicked out of seven countries because the government officials disliked my frankness. But each of these seven countries invited me back. They knew that a writer is never worth reading unless he expresses exactly what he honestly believes."

. Collaboration does not necessarily save time, and *Rascals in Paradise* was certainly not a rush job. The idea occurred to Michener about ten years before the book appeared, and he had pondered it for a long time before deciding that he could never work on it until he found a person who might share the broad task with him. The actual writing by the two authors extended over a period of almost two years, and revising and polishing efforts extended over five months. And to cap the climax, the volume was already in print when it was decided to hold back the publication date for six months to make way for *The Bridge at Andau,* a more timely Michener book!

CHAPTER *6*

Andau, Bucks County, and Elsewhere

A T CHRISTMAS TIME, 1956, a long letter came to me from Bennett Cerf, breaking the news that Michener had delivered to him a "powerful and revealing book" on the Hungarian rebellion, and raising the question whether the imminent publication of *Rascals in Paradise* should not be delayed to make way for the more opportune volume. "It is so timely and important that it would be unthinkable for us, as publishers, to do otherwise than present it to the public as fast as we can get it in print," Cerf pointed out.

I wired him that Michener should certainly have the chance to make the most of his report on Hungary, and a few days later got a long letter from Michener himself, sent from Vienna, giving me full freedom to express my feelings on this matter as forcefully as I might wish. "They feel that they must publish this book immediately," he said, "and there is no reason why they shouldn't, unless by so doing they kill off sales on the longer book and more expensive one on which you and I have worked together." The result was that *Rascals* was postponed until mid-June, and *The Bridge at Andau* appeared around the end of February.

I *Tanks Versus Homemade Bombs*

Michener's speed in reporting the fast-moving events of the Hungarian uprising enabled his book to be the first American volume dealing with this exciting and newsworthy subject (*Time* magazine's "man-of-the-year" for 1956, it may be noted, was the Hungarian Freedom Fighter). The volume was well received. John MacCormac said: "It may be too soon to embalm the

Hungarian revolution between the covers of a book. It was, in many ways, a unique event whose cause is not likely to be completely clear until we are further from it. But James A. Michener has made as good a job of it as could be made at this time and it would not be easy to find anyone who could do it better. In so far as he has limited himself to describing actual events, told by actual participants, he has performed a service for which historians may be grateful."[1] Wrote Walter Simmons: "Michener has told this story with his usual magnificent competence in a series of little tales about the little people of the revolt. Some of these people were assisted into Austria by Michener himself, and one even rode on his back."[2] William Hogan praised its strength: "Obviously written in white heat, his book at the same time is more than pamphleteering. It is a dramatic, chilling, and enraged document, made so chiefly by the author's disciplined detachment. Later, perhaps, the Hungarian story will be analyzed more thoroughly, but hardly with anything approaching the emotional wallop of this."[3]

A lengthy review by Emil Lengyel, author of *Americans from Hungary* and *The Danube*, concluded: "On the whole, Mr. Michener concentrates on the bloodiest aspect of the uprising, moving swiftly on the surface of events, paying little attention to the deeper sources at work. He believes that if the revolution had succeeded it would have veered to left socialism—not to capitalism. 'The Hungarian revolution of 1956,' Mr. Michener writes, 'was a turning point in world history.' It unmasked the Russians as brutal butchers; and, in his view, it is bound to have its repercussions not only in the satellite countries but also among Asia's uncommitted nations. Unfortunately, this prophecy has not been borne out by events."[4]

Resting in the fall of 1956 in Amsterdam after a tiring tour of the world while filming television interviews, Michener was not especially responsive when the editors of *Reader's Digest* kept cabling him invitations to cover the Hungarian story. It seemed too big a job; he spoke only English; he had never been in Budapest. But the strength of the growing anti-Russian movement in Europe began to impinge on his mind. One night in Paris he was on his way to the Folies Bergère with his wife when they saw a protest riot in front of the office of a Communist newspaper. "That was when I made up my mind," he said.

"I was impressed by the new bitterness and violence of the European revolt against Russia."[5] He agreed to go to Vienna to have a look. Then, "Like other writers, once I reached the Hungarian border and saw refugees, I saw in ten minutes the total dramatic and intellectual situation."[6]

He began work at once, and *The Bridge at Andau* was the fastest thing he had ever written. "I wouldn't like to do it again," he said. "I usually take about two years to do a book."[7] By the end of December he had sent to New York all but one chapter of *The Bridge at Andau*. But his pages were the result of a man-killing routine. He would leave Vienna about ten o'clock each night and arrive at the Hungarian border shortly before midnight, when the refugees would begin slipping across. Several times he himself went through the Iron Curtain to aid exhausted people to flee from the Russian terror. Two interpreters helped him in interviewing hundreds of refugees. "I cross-checked the interviews with two teams of Hungarian experts," he reported.

> When any discrepancies showed up I had still a third group look them over. I had detailed maps of Budapest and hundreds of pictures of specific buildings and streets. I made the people point out the exact spot where the incidents they related took place, and by comparing one report with another, I was able to weed out the inaccuracies.
>
> Some of it, I admit, was hard to believe. You'd be sitting there in a cafe talking to a mild little man and he'd tell you quite matter-of-factly, "I did this and I did that," and you'd say to yourself, "No, it's impossible; how could this little guy who'd never been in a fight in his life do this kind of thing?" But somebody did it. There lay a great city in ruins and a hundred heavy Russian tanks knocked out with homemade bombs, and somebody did it.[8]

The title finally chosen for the Hungarian book was taken from the central symbol that Michener had found to typify his story: "The bridge at Andau was it. It spanned a canal and when you crossed the bridge you were still on Hungarian territory. But it was that lousy little canal that stood between the refugees and salvation."[9] Over it no less than twenty thousand people crossed to freedom. Even when the Red border guards chopped down the timbers and burned them to keep away the hoar frosts of November, desperate Hungarians swam the icy canal if they could evade the bullets of the guardsmen.

II No Gaiety on the Danube

The first reaction of the reader of *The Bridge at Andau* is to echo Ambrose Bierce: "Can such things be?" The horror, the blood, the tortures, the mass heroism, and the flight of two hundred thousand last-ditch people from their homes—all this makes the mind boggle. For each group, Michener uses the device of focusing on the adventures of one representative figure or family —a device which intensifies the interest and the pain. For instance, the youthful hero "Joseph Toth" of Chapter 1 is a composite of three eighteen-year-olds who dared not give their own names because they had left relatives behind; they honored two dead comrades by using their names instead. In his final chapter, supporting the authenticity of his reports, Michener reveals the identities of those brave ones who asked that their own names be used to proclaim to the world their hatred of Russian persecutions.

Most of the chapters concentrate on one group, such as the college students, or the Red workers of the island of Csepel which was the factory center manned by the most favored Communist converts, or the family men, or the dead-end kids of Budapest, or even the child patriots who, able any moment to betray their parents into death by a word to the authorities, were taught at night to revere the names of the poet Petofi and of the the reovlutionary hero Kossuth.

Michener tells with thrilling realism of the first spontaneous outburst of October 23, when aroused crowds hauled down the iron statue of Stalin and eighty thousand Hungarians gathered in Parliament Square to listen to Imry Nagy lead them in their national hymn. He shows how the Hungarian soldiers went over to the side of the crowd and how even Russian tank commanders fired their cannons against the sniping special police of the Allam Vedelmi Osztag, or the AVO. He tells how no less than twenty Russian tanks and eleven armored cars were destroyed by Hungarian boys and girls, using only bottles of gasoline or merely sticks and stones in their bare hands. He shows how, even when the Russians returned on November 4 with Mongol infantry (the Russian regulars were considered too corrupted by human feelings to be able to fire on Hungarian women and children) to crush the new government's program and to "revel in revenge," the might of the Russian armed forces was defied for days by disillusioned Hungarians. Their leaders, Nagy and Pal Meleter, had keen kidnapped; but the masses published newspapers, carried on a tight general strike, and fought to the death or fled the country rather than submit.

Communist brainwashing of children had apparently not been entirely successful. "Hungarian boys and girls had been trained by Stalin as intensively as human beings could be to strike the enemies of Communism. . . . Yet when the test came, almost a hundred per cent of Hungarian youth hated Russia and tried to destroy Communism" (176).

Most painful is the chapter on "The AVO Man," in which Michener describes in detail the atrocities of the sadists who were put in charge of suspects and prisoners in the torture chambers of the puppet government. For ten years some thirty thousand of these brutal police and secret agents had terrorized the citizenry unchecked. And most depressing is the realization, as he says, that "Communism requires an AVO to perpetuate its system. From what I have seen of Communist regimes, I am satisfied that each Communist country has its exact equivalent of the AVO," because "it sooner or later runs into such economic and social problems that some strong-arm force is required to keep the civil population under control" (130-31).

Michener is always the supporter of the underdogs, even—as in this case—when the underdogs have been good Communists until they came suddenly to a realization of what Russian intentions were. The greatest significance of the Hungarian rebellion, according to him, was the fact that "It was the young men whom Communism had favored most who most savagely turned against it" (17). The people who fled were "the best people in the nation, the most liberal" (202). Furthermore, "It remained for the Communist terror, as administered by the AVO, to debase Hungarian life and at the same time to announce that this was being done as an act of friendship. . . . It remained for Russia to introduce into the terror business a completely new dimension: hypocrisy. . . . For this reason the AVO terror can be termed the worst in Hungarian history, since it did the most damage to the social institutions by which any nation must be governed" (144-45).

Characteristically, Michener felt that one good result of the rebellion, even though Americans did not support it by force of arms, was that it would make easier his attempts, in talking to Asians, to unmask Russian propaganda. "And the facts that we must hammer home are these: it was the intellectuals who led the revolution, because they had been defrauded by Communism; and it was the workers from Csepel who supported it, because under Communism they not only made no gains, they lost what they had previously enjoyed; and it was the Russian tanks, crudely interfering in the government of a neighboring nation, that destroyed the city of Budapest." But the simultaneous invasion of Egypt by several western nations, he felt, over-shadowed this lesson in Communism because Russia was able to divert criticism and Asians could only point to Egypt and ask: "Now you see what we mean by imperialism?" (260).

Michener's tone throughout *The Bridge at Andau* is one of factual, grim seriousness. There is no place for brightness or humor; this revolution is too intense for any glint of gaiety. Reading it is not a completely enjoyable experience; but reading and rereading such a document is important if we are to remain aware of the way in which the aspirations of a nation, to modify its Communism toward a less steely socialism, can be stamped out by all the might of a mid-century Russian army.

III *Campaigning for Kennedy*

The summer and autumn of 1960 were spent by Michener in pursuing his favorite sport—practical politics. The result is embodied in the volume entitled *Report of the County Chairman,* a personal account of the Presidential campaign that resulted in the close victory of John F. Kennedy. Michener, who found this election to be "one of the most exciting of my lifetime" (291), was—as has already been noted—a strong supporter of the Democratic side.

The press reception of *Report of the County Chairman,* as might have been expected, was far from nonpartisan. Samuel Lubell in the New York *Times Book Review* concluded: "Although Michener tries to make it something bigger, this book remains mainly a piece of campaign literature. Its chief appeal comes from sharing the author's own campaign experiences."[9] G. W. Johnson, in the liberal-minded *New Republic,* appreciated the anti-Republican shafts: "Hilarious, but very astute, analysis of the election. . . . It is Michener at his brighest and best. It is uproariously funny, but it isn't a joke book. . . . I believe that Michener explains more of what really happened in 1960 than all the solemn and ponderous analysts."[10] The *Christian Century* concluded: "His generalizations about the total effect of religion in the campaign, which are based on his own experience, are too sweeping and lack adequate sociological documentation."[11]

Most bitter was a political reporter, Sidney Hyman, in the *Saturday Review,* who felt that Michener should stick to novel writing rather than turn to political reporting: "There remains the long inventory of embarrassing defects. . . . There is an irritating air of condescension connected with his own part in the campaign. . . . The impression is sometimes conveyed that he and not John F. Kennedy was the 1960 Democratic candidate for the Presidency. . . . Finally, Mr. Michener's experience in the campaign was limited almost exclusively to the geographical areas that Mr. Kennedy lost."[12] Perhaps the fairest short judgment was that of R. C. Woodward in *Library Journal:* "As the national issues emerge from this personal, precinct-level revelation, it becomes apparent that this is not just the story of what happened in Bucks County; it is a miniaturization of the campaign presented in an extraordinary way."[13]

Michener found a list of reasons to convince him that Kennedy would be nominated and should be supported. He wanted a President who had shown he was friendly to literature and the other arts (19). He found a number of other good reasons, all of which caused him to plump for Kennedy before the primaries and later to accept the post of head of the Citizens for Kennedy Committee formed in his native Bucks County, Pennsylvania. But his deepest enthusiasm was aroused by the chance to strike another blow for the rights of racial and religious minority groups.

Report of the County Chairman is, then, not a rival of Theodore H. White's *The Making of the President, 1960;* rather it is another testimony to Michener's abiding interest in human brotherhood and in the abolition of inequalities. Again and again he found the controversy over these rights to be all-pervasive in the election. "The religious issue permeated every meeting I conducted. . . . Practically no one I met escaped the pressure of this overriding problem and, in my county at least, both parties were ultimately forced to make their major calculations with the religious question a foremost consideration" (107).

Early in the election he found that the fear of a Catholic President was widespread and shared even by some Catholics (26) as well as by Protestants (61). He felt that the anti-Catholic pamphlets which deluged the mails during the summer "ultimately reacted against the Republicans and helped elect a Catholic President" (95). In traditionally Republican Bucks County, the lines were clearer than in many parts of the nation. Michener's loving delineation of the people of his own region reveals the split. The "Pennsylvania Dutch" in the northern part followed the urgings of their Lutheran pastors to get out a strong anti-Democratic vote. The liberal, pro-union, suburban young people of gigantic Levittown were strongly inclined to support Kennedy.

Michener states that the main breakthrough on the religious issue came with the Peale-Poling report on the anti-Catholic convention in Washington. He devotes several pages to the support that the unions, Negroes, and Jews gave to the Democratic cause; but again and again he returns to the religious problem. On a tour of the Midwest, such intolerance aroused him to a speech he felt was "the best I have ever spoken" (249). And one of the main results of the election, he concluded, was that "Religious bigotry was dealt a crushing blow" (291).

Even the humor, and there is much, centers around such stories as the up-county churchgoing lady who, when asked in which party she wished to register, replied "Lutheran." Michener cleverly uses the device of reporting his dialogs with Miss Omwake and Mrs. Dale, two of his neighbors who with Gallup-like genius always voice the majority opinion on all topics; and both are firmly antagonistic to the shadow of the late Cardinal Dougherty.

Michener suspensefully chronicles his hopes and fears during the campaign. He was fearful when Senator Kennedy came out with the proposal to abandon Quemoy and Matsu—a proposal about which Michener shared Richard Nixon's doubts. Michener felt much better after the television debates between the candidates, but he was horrified on the eve of the election when a news story, later found to be a fake, broke which stated that Nikita Khrushchev had been arrested, deposed, thrown in jail, and replaced by Gyorgy Malenkov. In a heavily statistical final chapter he concludes: "I do not believe that Senator Kennedy won; I believe that Vice President Nixon lost."

The weakest part of the book is the account of Michener's barnstorming around eight states with a team of stars, stumping for Kennedy. He does not seem at ease in describing this shining company, which included Byron "Whizzer" White, Starlet Angie Dickinson, Jeff Chandler, Stan Musial, Professor Arthur M. Schlesinger, Jr., and various "Kennedy girls." He sounds strangely piqued by the remark of one of a group of Republican ladies at a neighboring table in the Boise, Idaho, Country Club, who pointed out the barnstormers with the words: "They're the ones who are going to take it away from us."

One of the most charming contributions of *Report of the County Chairman* is the delineation of the two Bucks County politicians, Johnny Welsh and Sam Thompson; these real characters outdo the imaginings of even the most skillful novelist. Recollections of his feelings when driving to rallies include not only exhausting labors in stuffy meeting rooms but also the evocation of crisp autumn leaves and a dazzling early Pennsylvania snowfall.

Michener's experience in his grassroots campaigning for Kennedy undoubtedly gave him the further taste for political blood that caused him two years later to wage a campaign for his own candidacy for the United States House of Representatives. The 1960 battles and the volume that records them gave him another chance to voice his liberal credo and his belief in the American freedoms. And, although the number of people whose votes were switched through the efforts of the Citizens Committee was tiny, it is quite possible that, around the nation, the efforts of people like Michener did sway the balance enough to give Senator Kennedy the fraction of one per cent of the total popular vote needed to inaugurate a Democratic administration in Washington.

IV   Rembrandts and Van Goghs of Japan

The student of literature can find much to enjoy in Michener's books on Japanese prints. However, since these books, which embody his lifelong interest in pictorial art, do not fall directly within the scope of this literature series, they will be mentioned only briefly.

The Floating World (1954), on which Michener labored for two years, is the most "literary" of the group, and in it he often uses rhetorical devices to make graphic and dramatic his treatment of another form of art. This book attempts to show the life and death of a particular sort of picture, the *ukiyo-e*, representing the "floating," evanescent, temporal world, which soon focused on the representation of the passing scene, especially that of the city, the Yoshiwara, and the theater. The rise and decline of this form in the period 1660-1860 he found to be a better example of the growth of a regional art than the Sienese school he had gone to study on his first trip abroad.

He states in his preface strong reasons why his fellow Americans should be interested in Japanese prints. But again, as in almost all his books, Michener's main reason for writing seems to be his attempt to remove prejudice and his championship of popular rights. The *ukiyo-e*, he says, was "ever a child of freedom and perpetually a thorn in the rump of authoritarianism . . . irreverent, disrespectful and an incitement to riot" (245), and reflected social change: "the irresistible upthrust of great masses of people from what used to be called the lower social orders" (vi). He defends the crude Otsu-e, religious paintings preceding the woodcuts, as the "gaudy poor man's art" (8), lively, colorful, dramatic, and immensely decorative. And probably his main motive in expending his energies on this scholarly book—complete with historical background, biographical details, bibliographies, and other apparatus—is to put in the hands of his American readers at a reasonable price a collection of charmingly displayed examples of a popular art, and to share with them his enthusiasm for it.

The Hokusai Sketchbooks: Selections from the Manga, an outgrowth of the earlier book, was published in Japan in 1958 in a style resembling that of a Japanese volume. It is an anthology of the best of the woodblocks issued by Katsushika Hokusai

(1760-1849), popular artist who died reluctantly at the age of eighty-nine, having published some five hundred volumes of art. Michener has selected the best surviving examples of 187 plates from the fifteen-volume series of the *manga*, or sketchbooks, issued over a space of sixty-five years. Hokusai's books were printed until the blocks wore out and had to be replaced; moreover, they were read to pieces by the citizen and his children. Hence the task of finding clean copies and of restoring their appearance was an exacting one. To the prints Michener adds an exhaustive commentary, even retelling legends forming the subjects of the sketches or commenting on the connection between a detail and some Japanese custom.

Michener expresses confidence that in the years to come the best Hokusai drawings will be "generally recognized as the equal of those of Rembrandt, Goya, and Van Gogh" (43), and elsewhere he includes comparisons between the Japanese artist and Breughel, Hieronymus Bosch, and Leonardo da Vinci. The author's devotion to his self-assigned task of recovering the best Hokusai drawing-books was intensified when he had to abandon the original manuscript during an airplane ditching off Iwo Jima, losing a number of irreplaceable quotations. But the rewritten manuscript again bespeaks his admiration for popular art. The *Manga* was "the victory of the common citizen who saw in Hokusai a rugged, peasant-type artist who created an art that he, the commoner, could comprehend and enjoy" (39). The efforts of the Tokugawa dictatorship to preserve the social *status quo* were thwarted by Hokusai's crowded pages, which to the man of the middle or lower class were his "history book, his newspaper, his scientific summary, and his treatise on moral principles" (40).

A third labor of love was *Japanese Prints: From the Early Masters to the Modern* (1959), likewise sumptuously printed in Japan. Most of the 256 pictures are in full color and carry the history of art over three centuries, including samples through 1957. Michener's ample commentary is supplemented by authoritative notes by Dr. Richard Lane. All the prints were taken from Michener's collection, valued at more than $100,000, which was later permanently donated to the Honolulu Academy of Arts. An expensive, limited-edition volume, *The Modern Japanese Print*, appeared in 1962.

V *Reporter on a Global Beat*

The uncollected essays that Michener has written over the past twenty years range in value from competent reporting of ephemeral topics to a number of pieces that have much more enduring worth. He works on all of them with concentrated zeal. He is almost equally eager to complain about Manhattan fire laws that deny painters a comfortable studio ("Should Artists Boycott New York?") as he is to pay tribute to Frances Sabin, a busy Waikiki bookseller, or to promote the coming to New York of Japanese theatrical troupes ("Kabuki is a Must for America").

Michener's continuing interest in the Pacific region is shown in several articles on Hawaii and its progress toward statehood, as well as by such essays as "Sea of the Talented Travelers" and "People of the Pacific." In this latter sketch he includes reminiscences of his assistant of navy days, John Burke, the hefty New York socialite who served under Michener on remote Rennell Island and who, to celebrate his accession to rank, put most of the staff in a borrowed airplane and flew them all into a Melanesian mountain. In this same article, though, Michener absent-mindedly places the Treasure Island of R. L. Stevenson in Micronesia, a long way from Captain Flint's Caribbean hideouts.

Nowhere is Michener's genial sense of humor expressed better than in the short piece called "My Other Books." Frequently complimented for writing volumes on the Pacific that were actually the work of other authors, he has become used to being asked: "Tell me, how did you have the energy to write *From Here to Eternity?*" and over the years has come to think of that book as one of his more successful efforts. When asked how he thought of those hilarious scenes in *Mr. Roberts*, he explains that he once knew a captain who actually carried a rubber plant about with him. On the more serious side, Michener has become persuaded that *The Ugly American* is his best effort. His most successful work continues, however, to be *Kon-Tiki*, even though he has now outgrown some of the theories expressed therein but still held by Thor Heyerdahl. He has become accustomed to being introduced as the author of *Teahouse of the August Moon* and of *The Naked and the Dead*, but he is proud that some of his admirers are still amazed at the versatility that could enable him to write both the *Bounty* trilogy and the music for *South Pacific.*

Among Michener's best reports on distant regions of the earth are those deriving from Asia, such as "Why I Like Japan," a country where "art invades all life"; "Facts about the GI Babies"; and "Islam: The Misunderstood Religion," in which he defends the beliefs of 350 million Muslims (not "Moham-medans"). His childhood daydreaming about Central Asia landed him in 1955 in "Afghanistan: Domain of the Fierce and the Free," and his article about this country deserves to be remembered, particularly for his descriptions of one of the lesser known nations of our world. His two trips to the Desert of Death were, in his opinion, the most exciting that he has ever taken. It was in this terrifying region that "one night when it was my turn to drive," as he says, "we were engulfed in a sudden swirling dust storm and I drove our jeep forty miles an hour headlong into a solid stone wall." This incident is recorded merely because his mechanic was able to improvise repairs from almost nothing and enable them to get to the village alive.

Michener's observations in many parts of the world also led him to decide that the "underprivileged" women of Asia, for example, were paradoxically under less of a strain than "The Hardest-Working Women in the World," the American house-wives. Those of other lands are not expected to act simultaneously as cooks, housemaids, baby experts, den mothers, politicians, beauty queens, intellectual inspirations, and active promoters of their husbands' business careers. Even with frozen foods and time-saving inventions, he feels, the problem of salvaging the young married women of America from impending hysteria has not been solved.

Well worth rereading is Michener's article on "Main Line," with its profusely illustrated presentation of the swankiest suburbs of Philadelphia. Going back to William Penn and originally planned to be an exclusive settlement for Welsh Quakers, the region became—during the golden era when Michener was growing up—one of the best-known social centers of the world, an Anglomaniac preserve of the upper set, and a stronghold of conservative wealth. The decline began, in his words, when "the show place of them all, Percival Roberts' palace, was demolished by the owner because from its windows he could see the tip of the smokestack of a newly installed public garbage incinerator" (39).

Michener's pleasure in discovering that these suburbs had been transformed by 1950 into the homes of an aristocratic but not baronial middle class (always excepting the skeleton in the cupboard, West Manayunk) is manifest. Michener mentions that he acted as a tutor in one of the palatial homes he describes so extensively, but the Doylestown orphan to whom the Main Line was synonymous with unattainable wealth never shows through his glowing account of this happy suburbia. He would be glad, it is clear, if all Americans had homes equally "wealthy, tightly organized, set in beauty, and jealously guarded."

Consoling to the widening stratum of older Americans is his "Report from the 'Frenzied Fifties'," in which Michener, age fifty-four at the time of writing, commented on the warning of a member of the American Medical Association that a person in his late forties and early fifties might expect to sink into "hypochondriacism, alcoholism, suicide, or even murder" resulting from frustrations and anxieties because he could no longer conceal from himself that "he has squandered his reserves of emotional, intellectual, and physical strength." Michener's wry reaction was to go around for a day or two waiting for the paddy wagon to haul him away and then, surviving after all, to query his acquaintances and extract from his tennis friends their methods for facing the growing limitations of the aging process. His measured conclusion is: "If in American society a man can live to age 65 without ending up in jail or the boobyhatch, he should consider himself a real success."

"While Others Sleep," the long essay on the Strategic Air Command bases throughout the world, which Michener visited and in whose B-47 jets he rode, was likewise a timely article. Conditions may have changed since, but his conclusion then was that "To win our war to prevent war, SAC must be kept super-armed, with nuclear weapons, fighting fit, ready to go." The article was reprinted in the *Air Force Blue Book*.

A recent essay that will not soon be dated is "Adventures of Men and Their Ships," in which Michener presents a sampling of his nominations for the great true narratives of sea history.

These include the heroic yarn of the *Birkenhead* disaster and the cry of "Women and chidren first!"; the masterpiece of confusion and terror that was the tale of the *Medusa*; the record-breaking achievement of the unsinkable Poon Lim, who floated on a life raft for 133 days; the story of the unyielding Gloucester fisherman Harold Blackburn; and the saga of the last fight of the American cruiser *Houston* in World War II. His final paragraph, telling of a giant wave that struck as he was at the wheel of a yawl in the tail-end of a Pacific hurricane, includes the memorable words: "And as our boat roared aloft toward the infinite sky, with tons of water cascading across the deck, I experienced a moment of exaltation such as I had never known before and may never know again. . . . All that I can recall is a terrifying speed, a darkness, a great rush of water, and a sense of God."

As one of the foremost travelers of our time, Michener should be heeded when he concentrates on the pleasures to be found in "This Great Big Wonderful World." He points out that eighty per cent of the leisure time of Americans is spent in travel, and he extols the simple pleasures that any tourist can find. "But," as he makes clear, "if you reject the food, ignore the customs, fear the religion, and avoid the people, you might better stay home." And beautiful as the great vistas of the globe might be (he includes in his list not only the island of Moorea in the South Pacific but the island of Alcatraz in San Francisco Bay), the people who live abroad are even more a source of keen enjoyment: "Superior even to the Prado or the ruins of Angkor or the sweet ocean road of Samoa are the people one meets."

Again Michener finds that experience is valuable in developing immunity against prejudice. "We travel to modify our attitudes, our prejudices, our blindnesses. . . . That we can accomplish all these things while having a good time is the miracle of travel. But we can gain these ends only if we savor each experience as it arises."

Although "travel is certainly one of the most dangerous recreations," it has many pleasures, as Michener fervently reports. And not the least of these is coming to the end of travel. "There remains," he concludes, "one pleasure of travel which is not usually extolled: the puissant, subtle pleasure of getting back home. In many ways, this is the loveliest joy of all." And in "A Present for Aunt Bessie," another short, light piece, he points out the futility of trying to save money by bringing home from abroad a gift which could be bought more cheaply in an American shop.

VI   *A P.S. on* Caravans

Michener's love of travel, particularly travel in Asia, was revealed once more while the present study was going through the press. *Caravans* (1963) is a novel narrated by Mark Miller, a graduate of Yale and the Navy, a Jew who does not look like one. He is assigned in 1947 by the acting ambassador at Kabul to find a beautiful blonde Bryn Mawr girl who, violently rejecting the smugness of a Philadelphia suburb, marries a young Afghan and then deserts him for a band of camel-driving nomads. The quest gives Michener a good chance to make use of his own adventures in Central Asia and to weave into the tale the history and geography of this remote racial cauldron.

The characters include members of the diplomatic corps, a fugitive Nazi doctor guilty of torturing Jews, some Afghans of the new and old schools, and the bold, independent Kochi sharifs who lead their caravans between Persia and India and camp in a secret valley not far from the Oxus for an annual conclave. The mixture of racial, national, and international types, of several religions and philosophies, again gives Michener a theme strongly underlining the slightness of even the most irritating human differences in contrast with the underlying brotherhood of all men—even though they fight with knives in a desert caravansary or clash beside a thousand black tents in the shadow of the Hindu Kush.

CHAPTER 7

Passages to the Fiftieth State

HAWAII, after sixty years of territorial status, was granted statehood on August 21, 1959. In November, as a giant-sized salute to the fledgling state, Michener's novel *Hawaii* appeared. For twenty months it remained at or near the top of the national best-seller lists. All in all, considering even such excellent volumes as Ruth McKee's *The Lord Anointed,* Marjorie Sinclair's *The Wild Wind,* Albertine Loomis' *Grapes of Canaan,* and Oswald A. Bushnell's *The Return of Lono* and *Molokai,* Michener's is the best novel ever written about Hawaii.

National reviews were laudatory, in the main. Maxwell Geismar wrote in the New York *Times Book Review:* "A brilliant panoramic novel about Hawaii from its volcanic origins to its recent statehood. It is a complex and fascinating subject, and it is rendered here with a wealth of scholarship, of literary imagination, and of narrative skill, so that the large and diverse story is continually interesting. . . . As this large novel draws into the modern period, and particularly in the World War II episodes, it becomes more uncertain in tone, thinner in feeling, and hortatory in its message. The writer who has described the first millennium of Hawaiian history with such eloquence becomes himself a kind of 'missionary,' or apologist."[1]

Mary Ross felt that "Mr. Michener has written a saga of the land that is now his home with the zest and freshness of observation of a convert, the particularity of a novelist, and insight gained, one suspects, from laborious exploration of many fields as diverse as geologic processes, the life of ninth century Polynesians, and the culture of pineapples. The prevailing quality of this book, like that of the huge Hawaiian princesses, is that it is enjoyable. . . . Strange as some of its people seem, they are real; they could have existed. Moreover, the book has the unusual quality of making concrete, through the lives of individuals, the impact of ideas and emotions and situations that are shared by the rest of the nation."[2]

William Hogan was somewhat more exacting. "Michener's characters are prototypes rather than people. As he has adjusted details in Hawaii's history to suit his fiction, the author is forced to adapt characters to fit into the big historical picture. And that is the book's main weakness. Michener sacrifices drama for pageantry, true characterization for literary showmanship."[3] Wrote Fanny Butcher: "One of the most enlightening books ever written, either of fact or fiction, about the integration of divergent peoples into a composite society. That it is also an engrossing story makes its message the more cogent. . . . What makes the novel unforgettable is not only the deep understanding of national dreams and ways of life, not only the exciting panorama of events, but the human beings who were the motivators and the movers in the creation of today's Hawaii."[4]

Horace Sutton in the *Saturday Review* was enthusiastic: "The subject is so well covered that it may be a long time before anyone essays another major work on the islands. . . . A masterful job of research, an absorbing performance of storytelling, and a monumental account of the islands from geologic building to sociological emergence as the newest and perhaps the most interesting of the United States."[5] Paul West stated: "Mr. Michener makes a very fine attempt at putting the primitive mind into modern English. . . . As the book unwinds into the twentieth century, familiar Michener stereotypes emerge, but Mr. Michener goes into them more deeply than usual; and for that reason most of all, this is easily his most impressive, most honest novel by far."[6] Even Riley Hughes in the *Catholic World* concluded: "There are some unpleasant, even repellent, passages in this book, particularly as the author reports the periods of sexual license in Hawaii's history; but the impact of the whole is one of integrity and courage of the Polynesians, New England missionaries, Chinese and Japanese who came in that order to form the major groups of power."[18]

I *Eight Pages of Ancestries*

Even in Honolulu, where cries arose from a few racial bigots, reviews were generally favorable. Professor William Huntsberry of the University of Hawaii, himself a novelist, wrote of the ordinary reader in the islands: "Whichever one of the racial groups he belongs to, he will be at times incensed, at times pleased; but finally he will grant that the completed portrait is amazingly well done. . . . Everyone in Hawaii should read this book."[8] But some residents of Hawaii, of the *kamaaina* or old-timer group, were horrified at what they feared was skeleton-rattling. They assumed that this novel would be taken by Mainland readers as verbatim history, and that the Visitors' Bureau image of the islands as a carefree Polynesian paradise would be shattered. Actually, thousands of visitors to the new state came because they wished to see the place that Michener had dramatized in his big volume.

Those who had lived in Hawaii for years and had read its history were probably least qualified to judge this book objectively. As they read the novel, they kept finding that it was not history. The book is not even historical fiction under the usual definition. There are almost no historic personages named in the entire volume with the exception of a few rulers; even King Kalakaua is merely referred to as "the last king of Hawaii" (561). According to the records, the first mission in Lahaina, Maui, was opened not by "Abner Hale" but by William Richards and Charles Stewart; and, at Annexation, the Hawaiian government was headed not by "Micah Hale" (579) but by Sanford B. Dole. The brig *Thetis* is not the *Thaddeus* that brought the First Company of Congregational missionaries in 1820. Michener's book is a pageant of the coming of the various peoples to the islands, and it is founded on truth but not on fact. As writer of several volumes of Hawaiian history, I feel that the reviewer in the *Library Journal* was in error when he called the book "truly a comprehensive social history of our Fiftieth State."[9] And yet few problems of Hawaiian life over the past century and a half are left untouched.

As Michener states on the flyleaf, "This is a novel. It is true to the spirit and history of Hawaii, but the characters, the families, the institutions and most of the events are imaginary." Disregarding this plain warning, and the clear realization that most of the characters are not modeled, say, on one particular missionary or sea captain but on a composite of several, some readers assumed that here was an exposé of a cherished ancestor. And as one long-time inhabitant of Honolulu once remarked to me, "I've never lived in a place where people were so worried about the reputations of their grandparents."

Criticism in Hawaii itself centered, then, mainly around the identifiability of the characters and the authenticity of the setting. The many other contributions of a good novel were overlooked in favor of these two aspects. Those who would never have troubled, for instance, to try to identify each person in *Sayonara* or to date the episodes in that novel were indignant that some revered Hawaiian personage had apparently been pilloried. As soon as *Hawaii* was published, Mrs. Clarice B. Taylor, Michener's research assistant on the novel, was incessantly telephoned by people who asked her: "Why did you let Michener say that?" The crime of the author was compounded when it often appeared that his presentation was plausible. "Isn't it true?" Mrs. Taylor would counter, and get the reply, "Oh, yes, but we should never talk about it!"[10]

Like Jack London half a century before him, Michener was condemned for publicizing nineteenth-century conditions in the leper colony on a peninsula of the island of Molokai. Now that modern medicine has eliminated any need for isolation of cases of what is now euphemistically termed Hansen's disease, everyone would like to forget those conditions; but those apologists who would refute Michener's picture of the Kalawao colony before 1870 might have a difficult job. And his references in this novel to other incidents or customs are frequently based solidly on documentary research.

Most of the criticisms voiced in Hawaii were far from displeasing to Michener. As he wrote me on December 12, 1959, he felt that such discussion ought to help accomplish "what I have wanted this novel to accomplish ever since I conceived it some years ago: I wanted people to talk about it in Hawaii in terms of history, sociology, relevancy, politics, vision. Nothing would make me happier than to have the book dissected page by page, for in the doing so perhaps Hawaii will grow up artistically. Then maybe we'll get the great books out of the islands that the islands have a right to expect." He assured me once that he would achieve his aim if his novel were superseded by a dozen better novels, each expressing the spirit of Hawaii as honestly seen by other authors.

That sooner or later some modern novelist would see in Hawaii's story the material for an epic piece of fiction was self-evident. In 1944, while escorting John Dos Passos around Manoa Valley, I suggested that he, as the author of *Manhattan Transfer* and *U.S.A.*, would be qualified to do a panoramic novel about the island territory; but unfortunately he walked into the propeller of a warplane on a Pacific island soon afterward and did not return to Honolulu.

Michener was a much more available candidate for the task. During his first lengthy visit to Hawaii, the longshoreman's strike of 1949 cut off shipping of supplies to Hawaii for 178 days and aroused such bitterness in the population that he was then and there inspired to write a novel about social relations in this melting pot of the Pacific. Four or five years later he outlined a plot to his editor and began serious planning on the book.

Michener's interest in Hawaii was combined with another interest—the novel covering several generations in a family. Chatting with me in New York in 1957, he mentioned that he admired the sort of book done by Joesph Pennell in *The History of Rome Hanks* and by Glenway Westcott in *The Grandmothers.* (The latter of these he mentions in *Hawaii* [723], along with Willa Cather's *A Lost Lady* and Kate O'Brien's *Without My Cloak*, as the kind of "family histories" that should be written to help people speculate about their home regions.) The production of Michener's own chronicle novel covering a number of generations in Hawaii necessitated an eight-page series of genealogical tables at the end of the volume, to keep straight the scores of characters mentioned and the some fifty-five generations between Tamatoa IV of Bora Bora and Kelly Kanakoa, Waikiki beach boy born in 1925. The invention of vital statistics of ancestors not even mentioned in the story was only part of Michener's painstaking search for verisimilitude.

II *Five Hundred and One Sources*

The novel that burst out at such a well-timed moment in 1959 had origins going back for at least a decade, and it required months of factual research. On March 22, 1957, Michener had written me confidentially:

For a good many years I have wanted to do a major, long novel on Hawaii and have had it outlined for the last three. It falls into five parts: (1) the coming of the Polynesians to Hawaii; (2) the coming of the haoles to Maui; (3) the coming of the Chinese to Oahu; (4) the coming of the Japanese to Kauai; (5) the coming of the Filipinos generally. . . . I would hope that we would see, through the successive intrusions of new characters and new peoples, the full range of Hawaiian history. The time of the novel would range from about 1050 A.D. to 1954. It would be as strong as the events which it covers.

Now obviously to accomplish such a novel I must enlist the aid of some good researcher, not because I could not do the basic research required but because I have neither the eyesight to do so nor the time. I therefore propose to employ, if I can find, someone solidly based in Hawaiian history and culture.

I proposed the name of Mrs. Clarice B. Taylor, who for years had written a daily newspaper column that roved through the many mazes of Hawaiiana. According to Michener's remarks in an article, "Writing a Book in Hawaii," her contribution as a research assistant was eminently successful. He found that she was "not only extremely wise but hilariously funny." Together they launched into a full year of study, and he lugged home with him some five hundred books on various aspects of his story material. Her collection of clippings was also invaluable. But perhaps the greatest inspiration came from long hours of conversation. "For this quiet little woman has an absolutely unquenchable love of the ridiculous, the absurd, the pompous-deflating yarn," Michener commented. "If I had dared to use half the riotous stuff she told me, both I and my book would have been banned in Boston."

Mrs. Taylor has published several accounts of her own adventures in working with a popular author. In "A Preface to a Novel," she tells of her first meeting and her skepticism about the idea of doing a novel in which the lives of the four main racial stocks in Hawaiian history would be intermingled. "His terseness was deafening. For a month we sparred. Finally I said to him: 'The things you want are not to be found in books. You are breaking new ground. . . . All this material you want has to come out of my head.' . . . Each time I said to him, 'You are the first,' . . . his determination seemed to say, 'I am going to do it!'" In the end, he also depended upon Mrs. Taylor for help in getting some idea of the Puritan doctrines of the missionaries, and he even argued with her when she swore that a marriage between a Punti Cantonese man and a Hakka woman was completely inconceivable. And perhaps the rollicking humor of the brown-skinned Pacific voyagers as revealed in *Hawaii* is directly traceable to Mrs. Taylor's imitations of the name-calling chants of Polynesian enemies.

Michener's method of getting into a story is shown in Mrs. Taylor's piece on "Michener and Names." She says: "His first request was for a list of about two hundred Hawaiian names, and a five-generation genealogy. . . . The name he liked best was I-liki, meaning the salt spray pelting a chief's face during a storm at sea. . . . He found 'Jerusha' among one of the aunties of a missionary wife. He knew at once that Jerusha was to be his favorite character. . . . Just where he found the name of his sea captain, Rafer Hoxworth, I do not know."

Among the five hundred books consulted, Michener got great help for his opening section on the geology of the islands from a multi-volume scientific work, *Insects of Hawaii*, by Elwood P. Zimmerman. He discovered much fascinating Polynesian lore in the publications of the world-famous Bernice P. Bishop Museum in Honolulu, especially *Ancient Tahiti* by Teura Henry, granddaughter of an English missionary; she had reworked her grandfather's copious notes, which were later mysteriously lost. The indomitable spirit of the missionary wives of Hawaii he found embodied in the courage under the surgeon's knife of Mrs. Lucy G. Thurston, whose memoirs are a permanent part of Hawaiiana. The heartbreaking efforts of the New Englanders to negotiate the Strait of Magellan were modeled in part upon the 1826 journal of Captain James Hunnewell of the small sailing craft *Missionary Packet*. Valuable illustrations came from *Dr. Baldwin of Lahaina* by Mary Charlotte Alexander and from *Historical Missionary Album* by Lyle Alexander Dickey.

Among the many pleasures of writing in Hawaii a novel about Hawaii, Michener appreciated the advice and assistance of the librarians of the many libraries of the territory; of the staff of the Bishop Museum; of the University of Hawaii professors of many departments; of the community leaders of Oriental as well as Caucasian ancestries; and of the people of Polynesian descent such as Mrs. Mary Kawena Pukui and Liliuokalani Morris.

Much of the background of the novel was drawn as well from Michener's own observations—not only in Hawaii but in Japan, China, New England, and the South Pacific. In order to refresh his recollection of the islands from which he assumed the first Hawaiians to have emigrated, he made another trip to Bora Bora. There he renewed his acquaintance with World War II friends, first met when he had viewed those islands under the tutelage of the greatest of Polynesian scholars, Sir Peter Buck.

However, it should be emphasized again that, although based on a wealth of background investigation, *Hawaii* is still a story of what could have happened rather than a documented chronicle. That the first arrivals in the empty volcanic chain of Hawaii came from Bora Bora is speculation only, and that they came because they were forced to flee from religious persecution is even more speculative. Nobody is sure whether the Hawaiian Columbus came from Bora Bora or Tahiti or the Marquesas, or from another Polynesian settlement. But the story is plausible, and that the Polynesians were skilled navigators of their hundred-foot double sailing canoes is beyond cavil. And Hawaii was settled by such Polynesians, quite possibly in the way that Michener so painstakingly describes.

III *A Difficult Man to Love*

Hawaii is a big book. It runs to half a million words—a length that seems even greater if one reads it, as I did, in gangling galley proofs. Its bulk impelled an Australian reviewer to term it "a relentless flood of a book that seems poised ready to engulf the reading public with the literary equivalent of a Pacific tidal wave."[11] Moreover, the novel begins in a way that any textbook of fiction writing would denounce as absolutely fatal: it opens with no mention of human beings, but with twelve solid pages of description. These cover the geological formation of the Hawaiian chain rising through aeons from a volcanic crack in the profound floor of the Pacific. Yet Michener again applies the principles of exposition in such a dramatic way that this section of the book remains a *tour de force* of popular science and was printed as a separate feature article in *Life* magazine.

The stage is set, after the lapse of millions of years of almost imperceptible evolution. But only plants and a few birds inhabit it. The empty archipelago awaits the coming of the various races which are to be depicted in the next four books of the novel (the narrative on the coming of the Filipino group was regretfully jettisoned by Michener when the book was already well along and its bulk was becoming too great to be contained in a single volume). Erecting this empty stage is a basic part of Michener's plan, for one strand of his theme is that the "Paradise of the Pacific" was never originally an Eden but merely a place where one could possibly be built by human hands. "For these islands," he says, "were a crucible of exploration and development" (15). Again, he apostrophizes: "Therefore, men of Polynesia and Boston and China and Mount Fuji and the barrios of the Philippines, do not come to these islands empty-handed, or craven in spirit, or afraid to starve. . . . Bring your own food, your own gods, your own flowers and fruits and concepts" (16). And in a sense the first-comers of all races were a band of misfits. "No man leaves where he is and seeks a distant place unless he is in some respect a failure," he remarks (70); but he adds that they did at least have courage.

Another and even stronger main theme, however, is the one Michener had used in his novels ever since *Tales of the South Pacific*. It is the preachment once more against race or class prejudice, xenophobia, pigheaded biases, and undemocratic reaction. Stated more positively by Michener himself, his theme is "the enviable manner in which Hawaii had been able to assimilate men and women from many different races."[12] The meaning of *Hawaii* is the triumph of Americanization.

To retell the story of *Hawaii* would require a volume the size of *The Bridges at Toko-Ri,* and I shall not here try to do more than outline the main sections and mention a few of the many special qualities that this big novel offers to its perceptive reader. The best thing to do with *Hawaii* is not to read about it but to read it, for the story moves deftly and clearly and requires little explication.

The opening section, setting the scene, is followed by four novelette-sized portions, each dealing with the coming of founding families to the Hawaiian isles. The first of these four sections is "From the Sun-Swept Lagoon," which tells of the emigration from the South Pacific island of Bora Bora of a great canoe-load of explorers led by the king of that island and his younger brother, Teroro, "The Intelligent One," a priest who cannot accept the bloody new cult of the god Oro. Filled with descriptions of ancient Polynesian customs and of the preparations for the voyage to a region that might well contain no land whatever, the narrative continues with a description of the daring navigation of Teroro on the five-thousand-mile journey until the distant view of a snow-capped, smoking volcano brings hope of a landing.

The discoverers name the new island after their legendary Paradise of "Hawaiki" and transplant to it their material culture, as well as their reverence for the guiding principles of mana and tabu. But Teroro soon leads a return voyage to Bora Bora, to bring back his unpretty but wise second wife, Marama, along with the goddess-stone Pere who presides over volcanoes, and a canoe full of children and flowers—all things that were further needed to ensure happiness in the newly settled archipelago. Slaves, of course, had been brought in the first canoe, but, mercifully, only one of them was sacrificed when the first temple was erected on Hawaii's shores. In a few pages, the earliest occupation of village sites is sketched. And then for nine centuries the curtain falls.

"From the Farm of Bitterness" comes Abner Hale, sallow-faced, puny, fanatical son of New England who, after hearing a talk by an exiled Hawaiian lad named Keoki Kanakoa, gets a call to missionize those distant pagan islands. Abner and his new bride, Jerusha Bromley, make the voyage in the bark *Thetis*, jammed into a tiny cabin with three other missionary couples, whose miseries, sailing in two oceans and through the terrifying Strait of Magellan, are not minimized.

At last, on page 206 of *Hawaii*, we finally begin to observe people living in those islands, mainly in the beautiful port of Lahaina, Maui, where the Hales settle and try to erect a firm church. The beauty of the location is lost upon Abner, whose ingrained Calvinism is at war daily with the polytheistic nature-worship of his flock. For example, Abraham Hewlett, one of his fellow missionaries who is stationed at Hana, loses his wife in childbirth because he and Abner refuse to avail themselves of the aid of Hawaiian midwives. When Hewlett is forced to resign from the mission because he has committed the "abomination" of marrying a Hawaiian girl, he condemns Abner and the others in these words: "You love the Hawaiians as potential Christians, but you despise them as people" (290).

Teroro and Marama, of the ninth-century discovery party, have been more or less reincarnated in Kelolo and Malama, high chiefs of Lahaina and parents of Keoki Kanakoa, who has returned there with the *Thetis* company. Their dignity is shocked when Abner embraces and welcomes into the church congregation a slave of the untouchable class, but they strive to understand and to enforce the strange tabus brought to them by the New England *kahuna* in the tall beaver hat. Keoki, their son (who seems to have been suggested by such historic Hawaiians as Henry Opukahaia, George P. Kaumualii, and David Malo), although a sincere Christian, is denied a pastorate; and he backslides so far as to marry his sister, the beauteous Noelani, but soon he dies (as did historic Kamehameha II) of the measles. Noelani then marries Captain Rafer Hoxworth, whaling captain and former suitor of Jerusha Hale.

Most of the missionaries, for one or another reason, leave the mission, which of course was not designed to be a permanent church enterprise. Scientifically minded Dr. John Whipple becomes a partner of Captain Retire Janders of the *Thetis*. Second-generation Americans, growing up in Hawaii, have to find professions if they wish to stay in their native islands. Intermarriage among Hales, Whipples, Hewletts, and Janderses creates a ruling class that will dominate the islands for a century. Micah, eldest and most brilliant of the Hale children, marries Malama, daughter of Hoxworth and Noelani, thus joining the blood of Bora Bora with that of the rising haole (Caucasian) elite. Micah becomes the partner of his father-in-law. Growing commerce based on sandalwood, whaling, and sugar planting creates stable fortunes for concerns like Janders & Whipple and Hoxworth & Hale.

The most interesting character in this section, though, is recalcitrant, scrawny Abner Hale, slightly mad from a kick in the head by Rafer Hoxworth, but even more mad through fundamentalist zeal that is doomed again and again to be confronted by the seeming victories of paganism, as when Noelani's prayers to the goddess Pele halt a devastating lava flow. Yet in the depths of dejection at his failures, even Abner can experience an authentic conversion, when his untiring, devoted wife Jerusha inspires him to preach a sermon which he based not upon the brimstone of Calvin but upon the compassion of Jesus Christ. Again Michener stresses that what we all need is an open mind and a change of heart.

Jerusha, indeed, is answer enough to any reader who might feel that Michener expresses "anti-missionary" sentiments (see the tribute to her on page 353). And Abner, extremist that he is, often wrings our admiration, especially when he defies the belaying pins and cannonballs of mariners like Hoxworth, who demand that the Hawaiian mission maidens continue to prostitute themselves in the forecastles of the whale ships.

Michener's attitude toward Abner Hale—although this figure, like most others, is a composite—probably reflects what he has said elsewhere concerning Hiram Bingham, vigorous leader of the First Company who battled personally against seafaring men bent on continuing the corruption of the islands that had gone on since Cook's crews had introduced venereal disease forty years earlier. Bingham's "self-righteous, unyielding rectitude," says Michener in his Introduction to *A Hawaiian Reader,* "gave Hawaii its formative character. . . . Hiram Bingham is one of the most difficult great men in history to love, but everyone looking at either Hawaii or the Pacific in general is required either to stand for Bingham, the bigoted Old Testament figure, or for those other Americans who almost destroyed the islands. I have always been for Bingham."

IV   Americans from Asia

The native Hawaiian race has been reduced to a tenth of its number since Cook's day, and labor is required to maintain the domains of the planters and merchants. Importation of Orientals is the answer. Thus the next two books of Michener's saga are concerned with the troubles and triumphs of the Chinese and the Japanese elements that were added to Hawaii's polyracial crucible.

"From the Starving Village" goes back to 817 A.D., but soon

brings the story up to 1865, when Kee Chun Fat, successful in California, returns to his Punti village in South China and encourages his people to emigrate to Hawaii. His nephew, Mun Ki, Macao gambler, makes the hellish passage on the *Carthaginian* under Captain Hoxworth. On arrival, Mun Ki marries a shipmate, a Hakka girl, Char Nyuk Tsin, who was consigned to a Honolulu brothel. They become house servants of Dr. John Whipple, who gives the hardworking woman a patch of boggy ground on which she can raise vegetables. This land is the basis of the Kee fortune, destined to become one of the largest in Honolulu a century later. As Dr. Whipple prophetically reflects: "In fifty years my descendants here in Hawaii will be working for the Chinese!" (456).

The Kee family beget five sons, all named for continents of the earth. The last one is born in the terrible leper colony on a peninsula of Molokai, for Mun Ki has been sent there as a medical case and devoted Nyuk Tsin has voluntarily gone along as a healthy *kokua* or helper to dwell in the houseless plain where gruesome creatures brawl unchecked and kill for food. Things improve somewhat after the Chinese couple murder with sharp sticks the ringleader of the faceless band of terrorists on the barren peninsula, and a primitive rule of order is established. The fifth son, Australia, is sent as a baby to Honolulu; and, after the death of Mun Ki, the faithful wife returns to that town, just as a priest named Father Damien arrives in the settlement of sufferers.

The fifth son disappears for some years, and turns up as the adopted child of the Hawaiian governor of Oahu. This lad, under his name of Keoki Kanakoa, is given some pineapple land that will stay in the family. All the boys become community leaders— Africa, for example, shows an aptitude for law and gets a degree at Michigan. Through practice of all the old Yankee virtues of thrift, family solidarity, piety, scholarliness, efficiency, common sense, and getting along with people, the Chinese community thrives and adds its customs and characteristics to the bubbling racial pot.

The predominance of haole prestige continues through the nineteenth century, however; and, among the proliferating Hawaiian-American families, two leaders stand out—Micah Hale, political sage, and "Wild" Whipple Hoxworth, rakish grandson of Rafer and Noelani. Initiated by Rafer at the age of thirteen into the delights of the bordellos of Iwilei, Whip comes to be a cabin boy on a whaler, a world adventurer, a scientist, a land developer, and a leader in irrigation, sugar planting, pineapple culture, importation of immigrant labor, and revolutionary gun-running. He is also a connoisseur of women of all shades. As his grandfather had remarked: "Anybody can be brave enough to love a girl of his own color." Whip is no coward.

His attitude toward the males of other racial groups, how-ever, is far from affectionate. He enforces fully the Masters and Servants Law of the kingdom, and he is the real enemy of Queen Liliuokalani when she is dethroned. Whip's interpreta-tion of the complicated Blount investigation is simple: "We may be in deep trouble. Since Cleveland's investigator comes from Georgia, he probably despises niggers. . . . As a sensible human being he'll try to compensate and prove that he doesn't hate other people with dark skins" (569). And the forcible re-enthronement of Liliuokalani by American gunboats is prevented because of her insistence that sixty American leaders of the Provisional Government should all be beheaded. The description of the bubonic plague episode of 1899, however, is a retelling of history much closer to actuality. It is this end-of-the-century event that gives the biggest opportunity for the Kee family, led by aging Nyuk Tsin, to use their syndicate or *hui* for further economic triumph.

Annexation by the United States, the not-so-manifest destiny of Hawaii, is accomplished through the wisdom of Micah Hale. But he recalls how close was the chance that the island kingdom of Japan might have swallowed the island kingdom of Hawaii (561). And the next section of the novel deals with the coming of the Japanese component, which arrived later than the Chinese and had an even harder time establishing itself under the patterns of Hawaiian and American social mobility.

This section is handled with warm enthusiasm and special knowledge, for Michener's fondness for the Japanese in Asia is easily translated to a championship of the acculturation of the Japanese in Hawaii. If the author plays favorites among any of the four groups he shows making their various passages to the Paradise of the Pacific, it is toward the Japanese.

"From the Inland Sea" and the concluding book, "The Golden Men," cover many of the developments in Hawaii during the twentieth century, among the haoles as well as the Orientals; but primarily the story deals with the decline of haole prestige and the rise of the Chinese and Japanese clans. Specifically, it tells of the family of Kamejiro Sakagawa, peasant of Hiroshima, who comes to Kauai in 1902 to labor in the sugar fields of Wild Whip Hoxworth in order to earn enough money to go back to Hiroshima. Stocky and courageous, for fifteen years he becomes successively hot-bath operator, pineapple cultivator, and tunnel-drilling dynamiter. He marries a picture bride, but not the one he had sent for, because on the pier he impulsively swaps his pretty, lazy choice for the sturdy bride of his super-patriotic friend Mr. Ishii. The Sakagawas rear four boys and a girl. Suspected of trying to help organize labor on the plantation, Sakagawa takes his family to a slum in Honolulu and survives as a privy cleaner, wartime barbershop operator, and grocer.

He demands that his children make progress through the American school system that is the best path open to them, and they try hard. Pretty daughter Reiko is rejected by the best of the public schools through the device of the "English-standard" system, but by athletic prowess the boys overcome their environment. Tadao is even offered a football scholarship at swanky Punahou, where "there aren't many Japanese" (713); but Australia Kee, Chinese, had crashed that admissions barrier twenty-five years before.

After Japanese war planes bomb Japanese people in Honolulu on December 7, 1941, Reiko falls in love with an American navy lieutenant, but her father complains to the commodore and she winds up marrying Mr. Ishii, thirty-five years older than she and still crazily peddling Shintoism and the banzai spirit. Her brothers, loyal to Hawaii, battle for the privilege of enlisting in the American army. All four of them serve through World War II, led by Colonel Mark Whipple, and two of them die because they have to fight harder than any other soldiers to prove their right to be called Americans.

World War II is a time of opportunity for the Kee family; they buy out the properties of frightened inhabitants of the islands who are fleeing to the American mainland. Still under the tutelage of old Wu Chow's Auntie, the Chinese reap a growing financial predominance. The war is, however, the beginning of the collapse of the tidy paternalistic barony of the old haole dynasties that have ruled by the interlocking of marital and economic ties. Hoxworth Hale—leader of the latest generation and head of "The Fort," the figurative stronghold of these dynasties— is a scholarly sort who did a bit of research at Yale on such personages in Hawaiian history as James J. Jarves, and he has by no means the completely closed mind of his cousin Hewie Janders. On military business, Hoxworth visits some of the other island communities in the Pacific; gets a chance to compare the problems of Fiji, Samoa, and Tahiti with those in American Hawaii; and also tastes the simple delights of Bora Bora, from which one of his distant ancestors had come. But he fails to understand his son Brom, a promising writer who is later killed flying a B-29, or to foresee the power that the Chinese and Japanese will have in controlling Hawaii at mid-century.

V Golden Men and Waikiki Women

"The Golden Men," final section of the novel, has been considered the weakest. The author, after eight hundred concentrated pages, is beginning to flag, and the statehood deadline is approaching. He often substitutes synopsis for scene development because he wants to cover so many more aspects of the events. The number of post-war conditions of life in Hawaii that are dealt with is amazing. These include the genetic perils of interbreeding of old families (809), tidal waves (838), need for land reform through taxation (843), the "modenne" girl of Japan (847), unhappiness of Japanese war brides of American Japanese (872), the incursion of mainland chain stores through the cleverness of a Boston Irish lawyer aided by Hong Kong Kee as a local "blockbuster" (856), the rise of the Democratic Party (867), union organization (860), terrifying shipping and sugar strikes (862), anti-statehood shenanigans of all kinds (887ff.), the McCarran-Walter Act (899, 905), the rise of Waikiki tourism (818), the "Cousins Society" (836), lack of intellectual stimulus among descendants of peasant immigrants (921), the Smith Act trials (924), the legend of the beastly whip-wielding plantation overseer (929), the survival of "spendthrift trusts" to protect inheritors of Hawaiian lands (910), and the further financial conquest of Hawaii by the Kees. The schizophrenia of the Japanese group in the islands is well demonstrated, not only by Mr. Ishii, who persists for years in believing that Japan won World War II, but by the elder Sakagawa, who finally returns to his native province in Japan but sneaks back to Honolulu because he is too old to use the primitive Japanese privies.

The "Golden Men" of the subtitle are defined as the present population of Hawaii, which might or might not be a product of interracial marriage but would at least be a "product of the mind" (807). Such a man might be "influenced by both the west and the east, a man at home in either the business councils of New York or the philosophical retreats of Kyoto." Each might pride himself on a high ancestry, real or invented. Hoxworth Hale might boast of being "pure haole"; Hong Kong Kee, a "pure Chinese"; Shigeo Sakagawa, a "pure Japanese"; and Kelly Kanakoa, loafing beach boy, a "pure Polynesian" whose lineage could be traced in the Mission Childrens' Library as far back as 134 generations (820). But they are all of mixed ancestries, and that is a good thing, for civilizations always accelerate at racial crossroads.

Throughout the book, ancestor worship by *all* the racial groups and the fear of contamination of the "purity" of the tribe or clan through outmarriage are stressed again and again. Teroro of Bora Bora, a thousand years ago, should not wed a girl from neighboring Hawaiki; and, in the final pages of the book, both sides of each family are ashamed when Judy Kee marries Kelolo Kanakoa or when Senator Shigeo Sakagawa marries Noelani Hale. The older generation always fights against this dilution of the blood, but the young ones go merrily on their way swapping genes. And the result is usually a more vigorous admixture that will some day make little Hawaii one of the greatest American states.

But as the final page of the novel points out, "in an age of Golden Men it is not required that their bloodstreams mingle, but only that their ideas clash on equal footing and remain free to cross-fertilize and bear new fruit" (937). Paradise is what men bring to it; and, in Michener's awkward metaphor of pineapples blighted because of a lack of zinc in the fields, the slightest trace of an element added to or subtracted from the sociological soil might make all the difference. "No man could say out of hand what contribution the Filipino or the Korean or the Norwegian had made, but if anyone stole from Hawaii those things which the tiniest component added to the society, perhaps the human pineapples would begin to perish" (908).

The weakest part of the book, in the opinion of many readers —at least Republican ones—is the "election of 1954" in which "Black Jim McLafferty's team of brilliant young Japanese war veterans" (935) sweep into commanding power. Actually, the Democratic landslide did not come until the autumn of 1962. Michener at that later time was able to crow: "A novelist is a man who looks ahead to the true depth of things. I was writing about 1962."[13] And certainly the young "Americans of Japanese Ancestry," as they call themselves, have more than made their mark in Hawaii. Two of them are in the United States Congress in Washington today, voicing their special knowledge of American interests in the Pacific.

One of the high points in the final section comes when Congressman Carter of Texas, investigating Hawaii's claims to statehood, refuses to shake hands with "slant-eyed" young lawyer Shigeo Sakagawa. He is told that Shigeo is really one of Carter's constituents; for when a bunch of Japanese soldiers in France sacrificed eight hundred of their men to rescue three hundred Texans of the "Lost Battalion," Shigeo and the other survivors were given honorary citizenship in the State of Texas.

Yes, the "Golden Men" of Michener's coinage do represent the neo-Hawaiian sociological type that is emerging today through an amalgam of seven or eight racial stocks in the Fiftieth State. It is indeed a land where a Punti Cantonese and a Hakka could found a family or the offspring of a samurai marry an Okinawan girl at a Congregational church. The one hundred-per-cent harmony that Michener desires is still a few years in the future, but already the lowly sons of immigrants have won supremacy in the economic life of the islands. The reviewer in *Time* acidly described the outcome of the novel as the triumph of the two-party system when "the barons and their one-time vassals all lie happily together on the same interlocking directorates."[14] The pendulum has certainly swung far from the days when one drunken German plantation foreman (665) aroused resentment leading to labor solidarity. (Today the Big Five has been replaced by the Big Two—the bosses of the all-powerful leading unions.)

On the final page of his big novel, Michener attempts a surprise ending more suitable to an O. Henry short story. The teller of the entire tale turns out to be Hoxworth Hale, who throughout has embodied the spirit of reaction. The idea is to point up dramatically the realization that even the Hales are among the golden men "who see both the West and the East, who cherish the glowing past and who apprehend the obscure future" (937). Most readers, however, feel that the effort to accept retroactively all the previous pages as the narrative of one of the later characters is not worth the readjustment. Such a hefty volume gains nothing by the addition of a whirligig ending.

Although the scope of the novel leaves little place for Michener's powers of descriptive writing, the spell of the Pacific setting is still fresh for him, and he even finds space to catalog the loveliest scenic views in the islands (688). However, the action of the book is so extensive and covers such a broad period that characterization suffers. The one million people who have lived in Hawaii since Captain Cook's day cannot be represented even by Michener's large cast. And with his cast of dozens, it is impossible to develop any one of them in the round. Several, as has been mentioned, are combinations of three of four historical figures or composite photos of types of persons. Sometimes plausibility goes by the board. Wild Whipple Hoxworth, for instance, is a grotesque. He stands for all the American enterprisers of the latter nineteenth century in the islands. Single-handed he develops irrigation, sugar planting, the pineapple industry, and even the importation of the succulent mango. He combines all this with world adventure, sexual athleticism, and the leadership of the revolution resulting in annexation. Uliassutai Karakoram Blake, the only character in the entire book who—according to the author—is not imaginary but "is founded upon a historical person who accomplished much in Hawaii,"[15] is the least believable of all.

On the other hand, such women characters as Aunt Lucinda Whipple or Malama Kanakoa of The Swamp do almost seem to be drawn from life. And Char Nyuk Tsin, known as "Wu Chow's Auntie," the Hakka woman who served as a *kokua* on Molokai, seems quite a believable sample of the Chinese matriarchs that helped to make that group the wealthiest element in Hawaiian society today. Endearing is her habit, developed on Molokai, of examining her skin nightly for signs of approaching leprosy—a habit she continues even to the day when she obtains American citizenship and dies at the age of one hundred and six.

Some readers have felt the outcome of *Hawaii* to be a libel on the noble Polynesian voyagers who first found and possessed our newest state. Elinor Henderson calls Kelly Kanakoa the "dispossessed," but he responds (830) that "I got everything I want" and that maybe the descendants of the Congregationalist missionaries are really the dispossessed because they have lost the God they had brought to Hawaii (837).

When discussing the scenario of the proposed film of *Hawaii* with one of the writers faced with completing that tremendous task, I found that he shared the idea that the ending is unfair to the Hawaiians. "Here you have everybody else winning what he wants," he said, "but Kelly Kanakoa, descendant of genera- tions of kings, remains sitting in a loincloth on the beach, strumming a ukulele." I tried to point out that Kelly not only was marrying a beautiful heiress to a Chinese fortune, but that he also was a golden-voiced idol among residents and tourists alike, and nobody could desire more than that. Elinor Henderson is not the only one who feels that Kelly is "the best thing in Hawaii" (821). Reminiscent of Alfred Apaka, whose death in 1960 caused universal mourning throughout the state, Kelly is supreme at doing all the things the Polynesian group has contributed to Hawaii. As Michener says, "the people loved Hawaii because of the Polynesians" (917). Kelly Kanakoa makes music and fun, he offers love and welcome, he voices the spirit that most of all makes Hawaii a paradise—the spirit of aloha. This spirit of unprejudiced welcome should long survive, for the Hawaiians and part-Hawaiians are the fastest growing segment of the present population of the Fiftieth State.

CHAPTER 8

How to Be a Writer

MICHENER SAYS, "I have only one bit of advice to the beginning writer: be sure your novel is read by Rodgers and Hammerstein." Actually, James Michener has scattered through his works and his interviews and conversations a multitude of highly valuable bits of advice about writing. His opinions range all the way from breaking into print to the function of literature in our modern society. A brief selection of these scattered comments should prove valuable to the student of the art of writing and should reveal as well the mainsprings of Michener's own achievement in the art.

Once I was present when he answered a drumroll of questions from an advanced writing class in Honolulu. For more than two hours at a stretch, without pulling any punches, he replied, frankly and unhesitatingly, to the most personal, probing inquiries. His opinions are eagerly sought wherever he goes, and he is generous in taking time to give them to aspiring authors, believing as he does that "art can prevent moral downfall; the totality of art, the whole body of literature, constructs a core of belief, of decency."[1]

Himself a late starter, since he published his first novel at the age of forty, Michener advises a much earlier blossoming, if possible. His years as professor, as a writer of education articles, and as a textbook editor did, however, serve to train him in what Dr. Strunk calls "the elements of style."

I *Foreign Lands and First Drafts*

Michener does not believe it it easy to tell anyone "How to Succeed in the Writing Business without Really Trying." He has warned in his valuable essay "The Chances Against the

Beginning Writer" that "There are few harder ways to make a living; there are few fields of endeavor which can consume so much of one's energy in return for so little spiritual reward." Then he adds: "But everyone is convinced he can write, and those who would shudder at the prospect of submitting an amateurish daub to the Metropolitan Museum have no compunction about thrusting their verbal daubs at the editors of the *Atlantic Monthly* or the *Saturday Evening Post*."[2]

In another valuable source, a tape recording of a lengthy interview before a college group, Michener stated his belief that no aspirant can avoid an apprenticeship to his literary craft. "I *did* serve an apprenticeship," he affirms, "and a very intense one, and I learned what a great many people never learn. I learned how to write a sentence and how to write a paragraph. . . . The English language is so complex, so magnificent in its structure that I have very little patience with people who won't put themselves through an apprenticeship."[3]

Despite his picture of the pulp-writing business in *The Fires of Spring*, Michener never worked on a newspaper or a magazine staff. Michener feels that a future writer should avoid a vocation in which the compulsion to write would be diminished—jobs such as newspaper reporter, advertising copy man, or publicity, radio, or television writer. He feels that university teaching is legitimate but dangerous because it encourages preciosity, delay, and faddism.[4] His apprenticeship came, however, from academic writing. But he feels that the art of character creation is something that requires an insight that is seldom taught in a college English department. "It would seem to me," he says, "that the one course in the English field that might be of inestimable value would be a course in contemporary literature under a professor who really bored into what the men were trying to do. I have had to give myself that course, and in doing so I found out a few things."[5]

To those who are "too busy" to write, he replies that finding time to work haunts every creative person, and that very few novelists in the United States make a living writing novels. "Think of the number of women who have written books getting up at four o'clock in the morning before their families rise. If you want to write a book, that's what you do."[6]

What are the chief aptitudes for success in writing? "Vague longings, the praise of one's family, and an apartment in New York have practically nothing to do with success in writing. A study of what can be accomplished in words, an above-average mental capacity, vivid feeling, intelligent analysis of one's own potentialities, and very hard work are the best paths to a career in writing. Nine young people out of ten are too lazy or too little gifted ever to complete the arduous training period. Never in a thousand years will nine out of ten who, in their twenties, vaguely 'want to write' ever do so. The chances are all against them. And yet, if I must denounce the idle, day-dreaming attachment to writing that is so prevalent, I must also report the magnificent opportunities that await the young writer with a true talent and the energy to perfect it."[7]

Michener has forsaken the attempt to keep a writer's notebook: "I become so immersed in the thing that I live it and breathe it and drink it and everything else, and I just *am* this book for the time I'm writing."[8] However, he does keep careful notes on structure and chronology. His very retentive memory probably obviates the need to keep card files; while doing a piece of research he can find a required paragraph even though he is using seventy or eighty books at the time.

The main reason Michener is one of the world's great reporters is that he listens. Almost nobody in this world pays real attention to what anybody else says. Michener has trained himself to interview people casually, without a notebook or a candid microphone; he *listens.* Two years after I had made a random remark, he repeated it to me in my own words. When he sits down to write, he can recall almost everything he has heard anyone say on his subject. In fact, he prefers to get aural information when he can. "I found he was like a Hawaiian," reported Mrs. Taylor, his research assistant for *Hawaii*; "he didn't want to read typewritten dissertations on a subject. He wanted the story told."[9]

He is, however, meticulous about checking all details, and pores for hours over large-scale maps of his locale. To assure the authenticity of *The Bridges at Toko-Ri*, he lived for about five weeks on one aircraft carrier and nine days on another; and his experience of the Korean War also included time with the army, air force, and marines. To check the multifarious details of

Polynesian, Chinese, and Japanese life, as well as of New England missionary life for his big novel *Hawaii*, he employed Mrs. Taylor, who later wrote in "Preface to a Novel" and elsewhere about his almost fanatical efforts to get every factual touch exactly right.

Although Michener has written much about foreign lands and has traveled more than almost any other modern writer, he feels that wide experience is not required for good writing. "I speak with a certain harshness on this point because people say, 'Well, it's easy for you to write because you have traveled.' I never heard a worse *non sequitur* in my life. . . . Writing is not dependent upon a vivid experience; writing is dependent upon a vivid imagination. . . . Most of what Dostoevski wrote about he never experienced. Most of what I've written about I've never experienced. But what you can do is have an experience trigger your imagination; then you're off."[10]

Like many professional writers, Michener does not find it easy to get down to the hard task of creation. But in later years, he has seldom needed to force himself to stay at his desk and work. "One of the best things I have is a kinesthetic sense. I love the rhythm of writing the second, third and fourth versions. I like to see the pages in order and I like to see the chapters ticked off, and I work to my own set deadlines and I like to see that I'm keeping within them. I love the feeling of getting it done, and that carries me on."[11]

He repeats the truism that if one doesn't stay at his desk, he get nothing done: "Even if things are going badly I usually stay the full time. My incentive to do the first draft—understand I have no problem with the second or third drafts—but to do the first draft my incentive is that I can, if I'm lucky, do four or five more good big books. I can't do any more. Time will run out. . . . If I don't do them now they're never going to be done. This is a very powerful incentive."[12]

"When it comes easy, the stuff is lousy," is Michener's version of R. B. Sheridan's "Easy writing's curst hard reading." He adds: "You write the first draft really to see how it's going to come out." The first draft is a "miserable experience" to Michener: "My connectives, my clauses, my subsidiary phrases don't come naturally to me and I'm very prone to repetition of words; so I never even write an important letter in the first draft. I can never recall anything of mine that's ever been printed in less than three drafts. I've never even released a book review in first draft."[13]

His first drafts are put down in as finished a form as possible, but without worrying where the verbal chips might fall. Nor does he believe that it is good to start a book by writing the easiest parts first, or skipping around back and forth. He does not usually rewrite chapters as he goes along, or read his previous pages before starting to work each morning. He may write an entire novel without ever reading the first draft, or the second or the third. But at every point he remembers what he must do to improve a chapter.

II *The Road to Bali-ha'i*

Michener has often commented on the need for many revisions. "I have never thought of myself as a good writer," he told a Honolulu interviewer. "Anyone who wants reassurance of that should read one of my first drafts. But I'm one of the world's great rewriters. The only competence I have, and writing comes hard to me, is that I feel reasonably sure I could do a good job of describing that table over there. Like all writers, I know damn well I can write as well as the average novelist. Without that vanity, I wouldn't be able to see it through."[14] Some of his passages have been rewritten seven or eight times.

Michener's rewriting is usually a complete recasting rather than a retyping that includes merely additions and emendations: "I almost never set out to do eight pages over on the third or fourth draft. I always say, 'Here's something that needs correction; it'll be easy and I'll do it this way,' and I start and pretty soon I'm in so deeply that the whole thing has to be done over, or had better be done."[15]

During our collaboration on *Rascals in Paradise*, both of us were rewriting the chapters until press time. In a letter to me on July 6, 1956, he said, "I find that three or four readings are required to comb out the clichés, line up pronouns with their antecedents, and insure agreement in number between subjects and verbs. It is, however, this hard work that produces a style." He feels that good writing gets no easier as one gets older. "It may get harder, because your standards are higher and your hopes for your own work are more profound."[16] But because his reputation will enable him to publish what he writes if it is good, he can overcome moments of doubt and depression with this assurance.

Michener is full of ideas and generous in offering them to others. After finishing *Hawaii*, he stated that it would take many years to exhaust the richness of the story material in those islands, and he suggested almost a dozen topics for future novelists of Hawaii.[17] In "The Conscience of the Contemporary Novel" he mentions five areas of American life relatively unexploited by novelists.[18] And in his introduction to *A Hawaiian Reader* he describes how he sensed a need for an anthology of Hawaiian literature and approached me about serving as co-editor, only to find that such a manuscript had already been prepared.[19]

Like most writers, Michener has several book ideas simmering all the time at the back of his mental stove. When he gets into production, though, he concentrates on one book at a time. He refuses to be distracted by trying to drive two horses in different directions.

Michener also feels that writers should never wait for "inspiration" to strike. His businesslike attitude toward his program is exemplified by a remark he made to me in New York in June, 1957: "I have three quite different books in mind, on which I could start work tomorrow. And I have no strong preference among them for the one I would begin on."

Michener gets up and works each morning from about 7:30 until about 12:30. Afternoons he keeps free. He never actually writes in the evenings, but he may do rewriting, correcting, or drafting. While on a writing task, he works every day of the week and allows nothing to interrupt. He does not aim to turn out a set number of words each day but rather to finish a particular subject. The best he expects to produce in a day is about twenty-five hundred words. Typing skill may be dangerous, he feels; authors who are speed typists can write so fast that their words outrun their thoughts and their sentences outrun their style. Instead of writing in longhand, he uses two fingers on the typewriter and just about keeps up with the pace of his thought.

Michener is able to do a writing job almost anywhere—in a hotel lobby, in an air terminal, or even in a plane. He owns a spacious home and a comfortable writing cottage in a tropical paradise topping a cliff above Pupukea, on the north shore of the Hawaiian island of Oahu, forty miles from Honolulu. However, during a decade he has seldom spent more than a weekend at a time at this Shangri La, and perhaps such an isolation would be too soporific for his active mind and social disposition. His novel *Hawaii* was composed in his bedroom in a small apartment in Waikiki, next to a modern high-rise building then under construction. The sea breezes were mingled with cement dust and the clamor of riveting machines was in his ear, but every week Michener turned out thirty or forty pages of first drafts.

Like most sensible writers, Michener refuses to talk about his current writing. "There are in the profession," he says,

> what we call barroom authors, and I could take you today to either Greenwich Village or the coast in San Francisco and introduce you to writers who are far better than I will ever be. They can tell you a story that has compassion and understanding and suspense and significance and the more they talk the more convinced you become that they will never in a hundred years write it. They're verbalizers, and this is a real pitfall for the would-be writer. I tell nobody. . . . Everybody asks, "What are you working on now?" The true answer would be, "I'm working on three marvelous ideas, two of which won't be worth a hang when I get to them." But how do you tell somebody that? And if you verbalize all three of them, you knock the edge off the one that might be good.[20]

Michener's usual style is deliberately clear and simple, although he has a wide technical vocabulary for the discussion of literature. For building a strong style, he recommends reading widely in contrasting authors like Balzac and Henry James, John Hersey and Truman Capote, or Dreiser and John Galsworthy, stopping frequently and trying to analyze what the man's style is accomplishing. "I suppose style comes out of our subconscious but we won't know what it is, I feel, unless we study consciously what other people do."[21] Michener himself has read widely in American and foreign writers. "I suppose that by 1932 I had read some eighty per cent of all the good European novels then in translation. I thus conceived my love for the great European writers: Balzac, Stendhal, Reymont,

Nexö, Couperus, Dostoievsky, Goncharov, Flaubert, and Alarcón."[22]

Michener said in 1951 that he would like to write like James Gould Cozzens (this was six years before *By Love Possessed* was published) or Robert Penn Warren. Of past writers he prized most Theodore Dreiser and Frank Norris, American naturalists of the early twentieth century. Willa Cather's realism also has appealed to him. He said in 1949 that Arnold Bennett's *The Old Wives' Tale* was for him the archetype of the modern novel.[23]

Michener's ideas on the elements of composition have been reprinted in college textbooks. A favorite is "Idealism Today," in which he even gives a sample lesson on teaching the structure of the four main types of English sentence. But concerning the art of the novel, Michener feels that the craft of composition is not enough. "Writing is not a collection of pretty words. It's more like architecture."[24] He expands upon this idea later: "I'm frequently approached by people who want to write. They always say 'I got an A in English,' and this is to me completely irrelevant. If one said, 'I studied architecture and I have a fantastic sense of balance and form,' I could become very excited. This man might make it because he has at least one of the components."[25]

Today, Michener is frank to admit that his writing is concerned more with ideas than with exotic style. "I betray myself when I say that I write nothing these days without the intention of beating somebody over the head with it emotionally or intellectually. . . . I don't have an infinite number of books left to write and I want them to count very heavily. I am not an Art-for-Art's-sake man, even though I condone this so warmly when I talk to others. . . . I'm didactic and persuasive and hortatory and everything else that a novelist probably should not be. I take my lessons from Balzac and Zola and Dreiser and that group—a very honorable group of preceptors. So I do start with conflicts. I do start with something I want to get across. I do start with some social observations that I want to make."[26]

Despite his disclaimers of hunting for Flaubert's *mot juste,* Michener's prose is frequently vivid. His titles are usually quite memorable. His second book, as has been said, bore the working title of "The Homeward Journey"; most readers would agree that in a line from Omar Khayyam he found a better one, *The Fires of Spring*. Other authors might feel it risky to include such uncommon proper names as Toko-Ri and Andau in titles that buyers might forget when they entered a bookshop; but Michener is willing to take the chance. Several Michener titles are so melodious that they were promptly transformed into popular songs like "Return to Paradise," "Sayonara," and "Bali-ha'i." (Michener borrowed the last name from a filthy village on the topmost point of Mono Island; he noted it down at the time because he thought it had a "musical quality.")[27]

Finding the right names for fictional characters is a fascinating quest for Michener. David, the writer protagonist of *The Fires of Spring*, spends a whole day trying to find the right name for a girl. Mrs. Taylor, in connection with research on *Hawaii*, has done a brief essay on "Michener and Names."

III   *Chances, Changes, and Critics*

One of Michener's finest pieces of advice to the hopeful author is his essay on methods of breaking into print. "The Chances Against the Beginning Writer" should be read in full. Michener points out that probably half a million people are at the moment writing a novel, and three times that many are submitting short stories to the diminishing number of magazines that publish such fiction. Yet, as he points out elsewhere, paradoxically the publishers are always hunting for good material and "the search for creative talent in America is unbelievable." He offers some hope and a suggested path for the aspirant who is willing to work: "The rule of thumb is, if you have written a novel, then it's easy to sell short stories; and if you've written a lot of short stories, then it's very easy to sell a novel—but it's not easy to do either one at the beginning. It seems to me that the short story, for the young man in particular, is a very good way to start. It's a fascinating thing, but if anybody could get three really good short stories published in the academic journals, the regional quarterlies, by the time the third one was published some publisher would write him a letter and say, 'Young man, you have real talent. We'd like to give you an advance on a novel.' "[28]

Once I asked Michener how he himself had first started to write fiction. "I had been editing other people's work for years," he answered.

At The Macmillan Company we used to be affiliated with the British company and our offices received a parade of British authors whose works were published as a routine inclusion in the American company's list. All of us were called upon to meet the ship and kowtow to these lions and were accustomed to watching them have a big luncheon celebration in the mahogany dining room on the top floor. I wondered why such a person should be honored so much more than, say, a little American professor whose textbook had earned a quarter of a million dollars. One day after watching one of these big-name British visitors get the red carpet treatment, I got hold of his last two novels and read them. When I finished I said to myself, "Jim, you can write better than this yourself. You just can. Anyone should be ashamed of himself if he couldn't write a better novel than this." And when I got off by myself, typing stories on a box in a Pacific island jungle, I kept telling myself that I should always be ashamed not to handle the language better than most people.

Even with Michener's experience and reputation, all that he writes is not printed. In the past he abandoned several books because he lost faith in them. He starts a great deal that he doesn't finish, "just because it isn't very good."[29] He wrote, for example, about a hundred pages on a novel about the Marine Corps in Korea. One day, when he listened to a marine captain tell the plot of a novel he planned to write, it sounded so much like Michener's own that he tore it up and abandoned the project. After that, he wrote half a novel about the taking of a hill. He even went back to Korea to get more data, but this manuscript wouldn't allow itself to be finished either. It seems clear that even the most financially successful writers occasionally waste time trying to do a job not worth-while.

Even as an established author, Michener is not free of worry when he has sent off a new manuscript to his editors. During the fortnight before favorable reports came from New York on his giant novel *Hawaii*, he sweated it out in Honolulu with all the doubts of any tyro.

Having worked in a publishing office, Michener finds that being entertained by the publicity department and given the celebrity treatment has no allure for him. He admits that, if he had not enjoyed success, he would go to cocktail or autographing parties or do anything else to establish his position as a writer, because that is very hard to do. But the main thing he does demand from his publisher is the best editing available. He told me once that he wanted an editor who knew more about editing than the author knew, one who could help the author see the work objectively and repair any slips. "You can't really read your own manuscript," he says truly, and insists on the most minute checking of mechanics of style and coherence.

He is eager for this sort of editing, but draws the line at efforts to tamper with his main intentions. "I am perhaps more amenable to suggestions than a lot of other authors. I know some who will not allow a single word to be touched and I must say frankly I don't envy them the results of their ineffable art. I think a lot of them should have been touched, real hard. On the other hand, I am pretty adamant in basic positions. If I want to deal with a basic theme I want no comment on that; but whether I have done it well or not I am quite willing to argue about."[30]

The exacting routine of launching a book on television and radio in New York is in Michener's opinion so exhausting that he avoids it as much as possible and finds that every two years is often enough. But, as he wrote when inviting me to share the spotlight with him in that city in June, 1957, he sometimes feels it is necessary.

> Yet when I meet with skilled writers whose books are published in absolute silence, and whose sales never exceed 1800 copies, and whose merits either as a writer or as a human being are never known, and who sometimes actually weep in frustration over never even getting so much as a single major review—when I meet such writers, as I do almost every week, I grow a little more humble and do some of the things Jean Ennis proposes. When you are through with her routine, Grove, you'll be spiritually worn out; but when you publish a book on which as much work has been done as on ours, and when you find no one paying even the slightest attention to it, you are not worn out, believe me, you are desolate.

The chance that a first novel will be well reviewed, if it is reviewed at all, is in Michener's opinion slight. Even the sort of criticism that a veteran writer might be given in the few, widely circulated review media is not highly valued by him. The tastes of critics, moreover, vary greatly. Michener still recalls the first two readers of the tales that became his first novel. These critics shared a small island with him and read his stories as he wrote them. One, a brilliant, acidulous officer, always said, "Michener, this stinks!" The other was an admiring enlisted man who always said, "Wonderful! I wouldn't change a word of it!"

Since then, Michener's attitude has been strictly professional. "Many people have asked me how it feels to read a bad review. . . . Apparently they think a man wants to go out and cut his throat. Nonsense. If you offer works to the public, you expect some bad reviews and some good ones. Neither kind can be allowed to throw you off your rocker."[31]

A Michener recipe to avoid staleness, which might be followed by many a professional writer, is to take time out after finishing a book and to give himself a college-level course in some subject which has nothing whatever to do with what he plans to write in the future. To rub one's mind against those of others, without practical, immediate motives, keeps a writer alert.

IV *The Function of Fiction*

As we have already noted, Michener believes that there is an element of luck in literary success, but that most of it is a result of hard work. Few people are willing to go through even the physical labor of writing. He worked on his novel *Hawaii* from 7:30 A.M. to 12:15 P.M. every day for ten months, including Sundays and holidays. Just to type, with two fingers, three drafts of his 500,000 word book would be too formidable a prospect for many yearning authors.

He also believes that the average author, unfortunately, makes much less money at his work than the average plumber: "The average first novel loses money for everybody, especially the writer," he states. ". . . Taking all the writers who could reasonably be called professional writers, the average income is less than $1,500 a year. I know, personally, less than ten writers who actually earn their living by writing. . . . Therefore it should be imperative for glib advisers of budding novelists to remind them that it is hard to find a publisher, that when a novel is published it is hard to get it reviewed, that when a book is reviewed it is difficult to sell enough copies to make money, and that when one does actually make some money it is usually not enough to live on."[32]

Even the rewards which seem so great are not always so. Of the $600,000 paid him for the film rights on *Hawaii*, Michener said that he would take home only $61,000—if he took it all in one year. Of the rest, $90,000 would go for agents' and publishers' fees and the remainder would go for taxes. The take-home sum, divided by the five years it took him to prepare and complete the book, would average out to an annual income of $12,000.[33]

Some of the animosity displayed in Honolulu after the publication of *Hawaii* may have arisen from a feeling that Michener was profiting by the national interest in the birth of a new state. He felt that the success of his novel was harming no one, and in a letter to me on December 12, 1959, he remarked: "I have recently been reading the life of Mozart, and when one studies the indignities he suffered I sometimes wonder why so many people are so incensed when an artist gets his fair pay. If Mozart had earned a little of what I have earned—all after an age when he was dead—we would now have fifteen or twenty great symphonies, half a dozen operas, and God knows how many string quartets. Who is happy that he died of poverty? It all perplexes me, yet quite a few of the critics seem to have been infuriated because my book was a best seller even before publication. I hope that the Mozart of this day is getting a little income, indeed I do."

Asked about his interest in writing other forms than the novel, Michener once said frankly:

Because there is such a dearth of dramatists in the United States, I am approached almost every month to write a play— with assurance of production, almost—and I don't, because I have no competency in that field. I don't think I could say anything fresh; I don't think I would be nearly as good as Arthur Miller, Tennessee Williams, or Gore Vidal. So why bother? I can do things that these writers can't do, and I take solace in that; but I certainly cannot do what they *do* do. In the short story field, I am rather hesitant because form is so important there and I write in a rather amorphous way, with big sweeps and pretty encompassing feeling. The short story form is not particularly congenial to me, even though I've had a lot of success with it. When I lie awake at night I never think of myself as a short story writer.[34]

Asked about his interest in working with film makers, he replied:

About nine of my books and stories have been or are being made into movies and I have never had anything to do with this process. I am not skilled in movie work. I am not concerned with it, and the first time I ever see what they have done is when it comes to my home town. I don't talk about who's going to be in it, I don't review the script, I don't give any advice. I've never seen any of them being shot. I do this because time is so important. Hollywood has a number of very talented people who have the time and I'm perfectly willing to let them spend their time on that and I'll spend my time on something else.[35]

On the other hand, Michener has probably had as much experience as any American novelist in the comparatively new medium of television. The series "Adventures in Paradise" which he initiated ran weekly for one hour for two years on a major network.

Finally, what does this novelist believe to be the function of the novel? In an interview in 1949, Michener expressed his idea that it should have a purpose: "In a complex and wandering society the symbols of art form a cohesive bloc. The arts keep a society pure, cleaned up. They are fresheners. They are a carbon through which society is filtered. Perhaps because I was brought up a Quaker, I feel keenly that literature must be looked at from the point of view of utility. For myself, I cannot see literature without a purpose. . . . The hope exists in this minute building up of fresh and humane opinion that is the function of art."[36]

In a speech in the third annual series of the Benjamin Franklin Lectures at the University of Pennsylvania in the winter of 1950, printed in a volume entitled *The Arts in Renewal,* Michener had time to develop more fully the theme of the artist's responsibility to society. Under the title, "The Conscience of the Contemporary Novel," he stated that we have entered the constructive stage of the literary revolution, and he pleaded with the younger generation of writers for fewer technical tricks and for greater responsibility. "They are fighting for the conscience of the world," he pointed out. "At a time when my country has become the leader of the world, I am banging on the table for substantial steak and potatoes because in this period of great hunger it is not enough for our artists to drag out pastries. We need, and we have a right to expect, substantial intellectual and moral food."[37]

James Michener feels, in brief, that the function of a novelist in our era is to report and at the same time relate events to the emotions of people. He is sad that, in his lifetime, poetry has fallen into the hands of purely esoteric writers; and he fears this tragedy might happen to prose.

Starting as a teacher of English, Michener the author not unexpectedly believes that the teaching of literature is now the most important task in the world. "Today I believe—considering how the school curriculum is disposed," he concluded one essay, "that the future decency of the world rests largely in the hands of English teachers. By a process of elimination, English has been left with the principal job of modern education. Literature must keep alive the sparks of idealism, human decency, hope, belief in a better world, and dedication to the goodness of mankind. By a process of elimination, teachers of literature have become the ministers who must see the world through its dark night of failing idealism."[38]

CHAPTER *9*

Area of Assessment

GRANTED THAT James A. Michener has not been sufficient-ly studied by the critics and that he is still writing and might produce books that would markedly change our present opinions, it is yet possible to make at least a tentative assay of his achievements. Here are a few conclusions drawn from contemplation after rereading about two million words of his published writings, as well as studying his letters and man-uscripts and recalling many conversations with him.

Michener's idea of his function, in summary, is to report the world, factually or imaginatively, but also emotionally and even poetically. And the act of writing implies the taking of some moral stand as well, even though "morality" is today an un-modish word. He fought to keep the song "You Have to be Taught" in the musical show *South Pacific*. He labeled himself a coward because he was persuaded to omit a chapter called "Lobeck, the Asiatic," from *Tales of the South Pacific*. His powers of characterization and description save him from selling his author's birthright for a pot of message, but there is no doubt that usually his themes are strong.

Primarily, Michener is not a born writer but a teacher or even a preacher. He did not publish a book until he was forty, and it is possible that his volumes, impressive and popular as they are, serve merely as an extension of his teaching activities. He is the professor *malgre lui*. In print, his classroom is the world.

His scholarliness often endangers his popular appeal, and there is a strong didactic strain throughout his work. His theme again and again is a variation on the Quaker belief in the literal brotherhood of man. Even in his fiction, from *Tales of the South Pacific* through *Caravans*, the main intention of the author is the exposure of unbrotherly prejudices—social, political, racial, religious. In book after book—even on such abstruse subjects as Japanese engravings—his interest seems to center on freeing mankind from illiberal attitudes. He is the friend always of the underdog; he is the foe of snobbishness, segregation, reaction, and bigotry.

Born with a keen intelligence, a retentive memory, and an urge to travel, Michener was early inculcated with a friendly religion that has served to shield him from deep doubt and to urge him to an almost missionary zeal. A deep-seated drive came from his orphan birth and heritage of hunger, which kept him from slackening on any job he undertook. He is clearly of the inner-directed generation. He was early the recipient of scholarships that aroused in him a feeling of indebtedness to the world and of a need to repay bountifully the help that had been offered him. His spirit of obligation to society is shown by his generous donations of time, money, energy, and intellect to a dozen worthy institutions, such as the Fund for Asia or the Honolulu Academy of Arts. He showed the volunteer spirit not only in wartime but in that time when it seemed he should devote all his efforts to winning a seat in the United States Congress.

Michener's mind would qualify him for success in several fields other than authorship. He enjoys the act of writing, but has mastered the craft by intense application, and his effects are achieved by calculated art, much rewriting, and a study of reader interests. His works are also popular because, when he is not in too much of a hurry, his aim is high and his achievement is great. But he early revealed other talents which, given the same development, would have brought him success in other careers. He won recognition as a teacher, and he was slated for an eminent position in the editorial world. Strong enthusiasms with him are the study of mathematics and the practice of art criticism. He has always been an amateur of practical politics, and has sharpened an uncanny talent for anticipating world events. As he wrote in 1955 for *Twentieth-Century Authors*: "In 1940 I lectured that we would be at war in the Pacific shortly. In 1945 I wrote that Asia must become our major problem and that we would probably be at war with China one day. And in 1950 I pointed out that all the turmoil in Asia would shortly be repeated in Africa. (My wrong guesses, which would fill the remainder of this volume, I have conveniently forgot.)" More than once he has been called upon by the American government to carry on confidential negotiations with other national groups.

Michener's trained memory, power of observation, and itching foot have qualified him to be one of the finest world reporters of our time—a time when travel has become America's favorite hobby and when no corner of the world can escape the journalist. Several of his books, such as *The Voice of Asia, The Bridge at Andau,* and *Report of the County Chairman,* derive from sought or unsought reportorial coups. He has been called "Mr. Pacific" and even "Mr. World," but his broad sense of humor keeps him from becoming pompous about his travels. "If I ever write my autobiography," he once told me beside his swimming pool at his Bucks County home, "I'm going to call it *On a Clear Day.* During all my visits to other lands, I never got to one of them at just the right time. The inhabitants always said, 'On a clear day you can see so-and-so from here.' But somehow I have always missed the most impressive view!"

Accidental assignment in World War II took Michener to the South Pacific, but it was not chance that he was useful in a task that required energy, mobility, and the power to get along with a variety of people from all walks of South Pacific life. And he was able as well to share with readers his knowledge of those lives. As Congressman Daniel K. Inouye stated in the United States House of Representatives on September 17, 1962, concerning Michener: "He is literally Mr. Pacific, a man who has brought the attention of the world to this glamorous, lovely area. In vivid prose, that has been translated into dozens of languages, Michener has told the story of romantic places, of powerful struggles, and of history that envelops us all."

But the author's exploration of the Pacific was extended beyond it to Asia. He is probably the person who has done most to make his fellow Americans aware of the dangers and challenges that the United States must face as the course of empire, taking its westward way, has come full circle and is now eyeball to eyeball with the East. Again to quote the speech of Daniel Inouye, who is now serving as America's first United States Senator of Japanese ancestry: "When I travelled through

Asia on matters affecting our Government I found that in many capitals in that part of the world, James A. Michener was one of the best known Americans. He had worked for many years explaining America to Asia and Asia to Americans. His books were loved by people who wanted closer ties between that vast part of the world and the United States. The popular motion pictures that showed Asia to the rest of the world were enjoyed in these capitals. But most of all I found men and women of Asia knew Michener for the large number of books and articles he had written about the serious problems in this continent."

Michener's amazing versatility in type of publication has been mentioned in Chapter 1. From the start he resisted the temptation to follow up a former success. His name is almost as well known on stage, film, and television announcements as it is in the columns of *Publisher's Weekly*. But he himself feels that his main achievement has been in the short story, and even more in the novel.

Aside from a handful of masterly short stories, such as "A Boar's Tooth," "Our Heroine," "Fo' Dolla'," "The Cave," "Mutiny," "Wine for the Mess at Segi," "Mr. Morgan," and "Povenaaa's Daughter"—a list impressive enough to make a reputation for anyone—Michener's greatest contribution so far has been in the genre of the novel. *Tales of the South Pacific* is, all things considered, the best novel to come out of the World War II conflict in the Pacific. *Hawaii* is, all things considered, the best novel yet written about the genesis of America's newest state.

A final query comes to mind: Can we classify this novelist among the usual critical categories? Although Michener has studied and admired the great European novelists, it is clear that he himself is deep in the American tradition. He speaks respectfully of such early twentieth-century American naturalists as Theodore Dreiser and Frank Norris; and he is aware of the current of naturalism that descended to them from Zola and Flaubert. Is Michener a naturalist?

If we apply the usual Parringtonian criteria of objectivity, frankness, amorality, determinism, pessimism, and a resultant bias in character selection, it seems obvious that the label will not fit. Michener in his author stance is closer to the soap box than to the laboratory of the social scientist. He is highly moral and confessedly optimistic, and is committed to a faith in progress and the rational improvability of man. His characters are often chosen or molded to enact his theme, but seldom does he offer for our admiration a "hairy ape" with strong back and weak mind, or a Strindbergian neurotic, or an alcoholic, dope-riddled, epicene anti-hero, or a flabby victim of "circumstance" or "society" in a world he never even tried to make. Michener is frank to the point of horrifying some of his otherwise adoring readers, but frankness is expected nowadays in any novel that does not wish to be damned as Victorian.

No, Michener is perhaps less close to the naturalists than to the "muckrakers" of the early period—those crusaders like Jack London and Upton Sinclair who found in fiction a broader extension of their revelatory reportage. And perhaps he is most of all the contemporary reporter, in fiction as well as fact—one of the noble, articulate band of rovers that keep showing our generation what we are really like. After all, John Steinbeck and John Hersey have made literature of suffering and injustice and prejudice and courage; and all of his life Ernest Hemingway never disdained the proud title of reporter. So long as modern Americans need to know who they are, in a world of wars hot and cold, so long will Michener's books be read.

Notes and References

Chapter One

1. "VII. Edwin Joseph Michener was born 2-20-1876. He married 7-7-1900 Mabel Haddock. She was a daughter of Robert and Kate Haddock. He died 3-17-1902. She died 3-22-1946. *Children:* Robert Ezra, born 10-23-1901. James Albert (adopted), 2-3-1907."—Anna E. Shaddinger, *The Micheners in America* (Tokyo, 1958).

2. *Report of the County Chairman* (New York, 1961), p. 244.

3. New York *Times,* February 3, 1947, p. 17.

4. New York *Times,* December 24, 1956, p. 4.

5. "Report from the Frenzied Fifties," New York *Times Magazine,* August 13, 1961, p. 96.

6. *Report of the County Chairman,* p. 9.

7. Honolulu *Star-Bulletin,* November 17, 1959, p. 1B.

8. *Saturday Evening Post,* CCXXXV (May 5, 1962), 8. Reprinted by special permission, © 1962, the Curtis Publishing Co.

9. Honolulu Sunday *Star-Bulletin and Advertiser,* September 23, 1962.

Chapter Two

1. Bob Krauss, "Success Story of a Story," *Paradise of the Pacific,* Honolulu, LXXI (November, 1959), 157.

2. February 2, 1947, VII, 5.

3. XXXVI (Spring, 1947), 576.

4. Krauss, *op cit.*

5. May 16, 1948, VII, 8.

6. The narrator appears in thirteen of the nineteen sections. Tony Fry appears in nine; Bus Adams, in six; Harbison, in five; Billis and Dr. Benoway, in four each; and Joe Cable, in two. Of the women, Latouche De Becque appears in three and Nellie Forbush in two. Admiral Kester is often onstage or in the wings.

7. The officer-narrator tells thirteen of the tales. Bus Adams tells "The Milk Run" and "Those Who Fraternize." An omniscient narrator gives us "An Officer and a Gentleman," "Our Heroine," "Dry Rot," and "Passion."

8. This incident is used as a climactic one in the musical play *South Pacific*—in it, however, the "big dealer" Luther Billis causes the navy tremendous trouble.

9. Prophetically, a decade before Little Rock became synonymous around the world with racial prejudice, the region was selected by Michener as the place of Nellie's origin.

10. "Happy Talk," New York *Times,* July 3, 1949, II, 1.

11. New York *Times,* September 23, 1956, II, 1.

12. "Happy Talk," *op. cit.*

13. New York *Times,* May 16, VII, 8.

14. "Biographical Note," *Saturday Review of Literature,* XXXIV (April 28, 1951), 10. Appreciation of Norman Mailer's book is greatly tarnished by the revelation that it is a Marxist allegory hewing to the party line (see Robert Lee Scott, *"The Naked and the Dead: A Tour de Force,"* University of Hawaii Thesis for Degree of Master of Arts, No. 302, Honolulu, 1953, typescript).

Chapter Three

1. *Return to Paradise* (New York, 1951), p. 3.

2. "I Would Not Minimize That Apprenticeship . . ." *Northwest Review,* IV (Spring, 1961), 7.

3. *Report of the County Chairman* (New York, 1961), p. 4.

4. *Yale Review* ns, XXXVIII (Spring, 1949), 574.

5. *Library Journal,* LXXIV (January 1, 1949), 60.

6. New York *Times,* February 6, 1949, p. 7.

7. *Christian Science Monitor,* February 15, 1949, p. 12.

8. CLXXIII (August, 1951), 390.

9. May 6, 1951, p. 3.

10. *Commonweal,* LIV (April 27, 1951), 67.

11. *Saturday Review of Literature,* XXXIV (April 28, 1951), 10.

12. See, for example, his introduction to *The Spell of the Pacific,* edited by Carl Stroven and A. Grove Day (New York, 1949), and his essay, "Sea of the Talented Traveler," *Saturday Review,* XXXVII (October 23, 1954), 47-48.

13. Any resemblance to Harry Brunner, pilot hero of Wolfert's *Act of Love,* is probably coincidental. The main character of Michener's *The Bridges at Toko-Ri* is a flyer named Harry Brubaker.

14. A fairly good estimate: in 1963 the best population figures for the Crown Colony showed about 213,000 Indians, 178,00 Fijians, and 37,000 others.

Chapter Four

1. *Library Journal,* LXXVI (November 15, 1951), 1932.

2. New York *Herald-Tribune Book Review,* October 28, 1951, p. 5.

3. New York *Times,* October 28, 1951, p. 6.

4. *Selected Writings* (New York, 1957), p. x.

5. "Talk with Mr. Michener," New York *Times Book Review,* July 12, 1953, VII, 16.

6. *Catholic World,* CLXXVIII (October, 1953), 71.

7. New York *Herald-Tribune Book Review,* July 12, 1953, p. 1.

8. XXXVI (July 11, 1953), 22.

9. *New Republic,* CXXIX (August 17, 1953), 20.

10. New York *Times Book Review,* July 12, 1953, p. 5.

11. New York *Times,* July 2, 1953, p. 21.

12. New York *Herald-Tribune Book Review,* January 24, 1954, p. 4.

13. *Spectator* (June 25, 1954).

14. *Saturday Review,* XXXVII (February 6, 1954), 11.

15. Chicago *Sunday Tribune,* January 31, 1954, p. 3.

16. Prints of Hana-ogi by the artist Utamaro are to be found in Plate 53 of Michener's *The Floating World* (New York, 1955) and Plate 163 of his *Japanese Prints* (Tokyo, 1959). In the latter book he remarks: "It was from my account of this haunting woman that I was able to afford most of the prints shown here, so in a very real sense she can be called the patron saint of this collection, except that the word saint is one which hardly applies to this remarkable woman" (142).

Chapter Five

1. XL (June 8, 1957), 33.

2. New York *Herald-Tribune,* June 10, 1957, p. 15.

3. New York *Times,* June 22, 1957, p. 13.

4. New York *Herald-Tribune Book Review,* June 16, 1957, p. 1.

5. Chicago *Sunday Tribune,* June 23, 1957, p. 3.

6. Chicago *Sun Times,* June 9, 1957.

7. San Francisco *Chronicle,* June 11, 1957, p. 21.

8. LXXXII (June 15, 1957), 1672.

9. Our method was not too different from that used by Nordhoff and Hall while writing *Mutiny on the "Bounty,"* as described in a letter from Hall to Dr. Chilson H. Leonard of The Phillips Exeter Academy, Exeter, New Hampshire, January 5, 1935: "When we had done our preliminary reading, we of course talked the story over, from every possible point of view, and decided what our method of telling it should be. . . . When it came to the task of writing, we divided the story into chapters, each of us taking those which most appealed to him. Then, the first draft completed,

we exchanged work, each man criticising and making suggestions before we did our revising. Throughout the trilogy each chapter is largely the work of one or the other of us, although there are certain paragraphs, sentences, and fragments of sentences written in collaboration."

10. The various versions of the *Rascals in Paradise* manuscript, along with our correspondence on the writing of it, are housed in the Hawaiian Collection of the Gregg M. Sinclair Library of the University of Hawaii and may be examined by researchers.

11. Captain Joshua Slocum's visit to Manila (243) was not made in the yacht *Spray* but in another vessel.

Chapter Six

1. New York *Times*, March 3, 1957, p. 1.
2. Chicago *Sunday Tribune*, March 3, 1957, p. 1.
3. San Francisco *Chronicle*, February 28, 1957, p. 23.
4. *Saturday Review*, XL (March 2, 1957), 13.
5. "An Author Explains," *Newsweek*, March 4, 1957, 104-5.
6. *Ibid.*
7. Robert Clurman, "Talk with Mr. Michener," New York *Times Book Review*, March 3, 1957, VII, 18.
8. *Ibid.*
9. June 18, 1961, p. 12.
10. CXLIV (May 29, 1961), 144.
11. LXXVIII (June 28, 1961).
12. XLIV (June 10, 1961), 42.
13. LXXXVI (June 1, 1961), 2112.

Chapter Seven

1. November 22, 1959, p. 4.
2. New York *Herald-Tribune Book Review*, November 22, 1959, p. 3.
3. San Francisco *Chronicle*, November 24, 1959, p. 39.
4. Chicago Sunday *Tribune*, November 22, 1959, p. 1.
5. XLII (November 21, 1959), 40.
6. *New Statesman*, LIX (June 25, 1960), 95.
7. CXCI (June, 1960), 185.
8. Honolulu *Advertiser*, October 25, 1959, p. A23.
9. LXXXIV (December 15, 1959), 3870.
10. Honolulu *Star-Bulletin*, July 28, 1961, p. 18.

11. Terry Chapman in Sydney *Morning Herald,* September 17, 1960, p. 15.

12. *Report of the County Chairman* (New York, 1960), p. 9.

13. Letter in Honolulu *Star-Bulletin,* November 13, 1962.

14. LXXIV (November 23, 1959), 107.

15. See flyleaf of novel.

Chapter Eight

1. J. K. Hutchins, "On an Author," New York *Herald-Tribune Books,* May 20, 1951, p. 3.

2. Page 103. Hereinafter cited as "Chances."

3. "I Would Not Minimize That Apprenticeship . . ." *Northwest Review,* IV (Spring, 1961), 8. Hereinafter cited as "Apprenticeship."

4. "Apprenticeship," pp. 19-20.

5. *Ibid.,* p. 5.

6. *Ibid.,* p. 6.

7. "Chances," p. 109.

8. "Apprenticeship," p. 11.

9. "A Preface to a Novel," Honolulu *Star-Bulletin,* June 5, 1960, Hawaiian Life supplement, p. 3.

10. "Apprenticeship," p. 14.

11. *Ibid.,* p. 11.

12. *Ibid.,* p. 12.

13. *Ibid.,* pp. 8-9.

14. Bob Krauss, "Success Story of a Story," *Paradise of the Pacific,* Honolulu, LXXI (November, 1959), 157.

15. "Apprenticeship," p. 13.

16. *Ibid.,* p. 28.

17. "Writing a Book in Hawaii," *Paradise of the Pacific,* Honolulu, LXXI (November, 1959), 156.

18. "The Conscience of the Contemporary Novel," in *The Arts in Renewal* (Philadelphia, 1951), 123.

19. Page xii.

20. "Apprenticeship," p. 20.

21. *Ibid.,* p. 18.

22. "Idealism Today," *High Points,* XXXI (May, 1949), 14.

23. Harvey Breit, "Talk with Mr. Michener," New York *Times,* May 22, 1949, p. 26.

24. "Apprenticeship," p. 12.

25. *Ibid.,* p. 19.

26. *Ibid.,* p. 16.

27. *Return to Paradise* (New York, 1951), p. 177.

28. "Apprenticeship," p. 21.
29. *Ibid.*, p. 23.
30. *Ibid.*, p. 23.
31. Honolulu *Advertiser,* October 13, 1959, p. B3.
32. "Chances," p. 106.
33. See Note 14 above.
34. "Apprenticeship," p. 21.
35. *Ibid.*, pp. 26-27.
36. See Note 23 above.
37. See Note 17 above, p. 122.
38. "Idealism Today," *High Points*, XXXI (May, 1949), 21.

Selected Bibliography

PRIMARY SOURCES

Because no published bibliography exists through 1962, an attempt has been made to be fairly complete here, at the risk of including fugitive items. The many foreign editions of works are, however, omitted, as well as selections in college anthologies and rhetorics. The help of the Swarthmore College Library in checking this bibliography with its collection of Michener items is gratefully acknowledged.

1. Collections

Selected Writings, with a preface by the author. New York: Random House, Modern Library, 1957. Includes Foreword; "Our Heroine," "A Boar's Tooth" (from *Tales of the South Pacific*); "Mr. Morgan," "Povenaaa's Daughter," "The Mynah Birds," "The Fossickers" (from *Return to Paradise*); 13 selections from *The Voice of Asia*); *The Bridges at Toko-Ri* (complete).

2. Books

Tales of the South Pacific. New York: Macmillan, 1947. Bantam Books (paperbound, abridged), 1948; (unabridged), 1957. Serial publication: "Best Man in de Navy," *Saturday Evening Post,* CCXIX (January 18, 1947), 18-19; "Remittance Man," *Saturday Evening Post,* CCXIX (December 14, 1946), 16-17. Collected: "Airstrip at Konora," in C. A. Fenton, *Best Short Stories of World War II,* New York: Viking, 1957; "A Boar's Tooth," in C. Stead, *Great Stories of the South Sea Islands,* New York: Saunders, 1956; "The Cave," in Orville Prescott, *Mid-Century,* New York: Pocket Books, 1959; "Landing on Kuralei," in G. C. Aymar, *Treasury of Sea Stories,* New York: Barnes, 1948; "Milk Run," in P. Jensen, *Fireside Book of Flying Stories,* New York: Simon & Schuster, 1951, also in *Reader's Digest* LVI (June, 1950), 57-60; "Mutiny," in A. Grove Day and Carl Stroven, *Best South Sea Stories,* New York: Appleton-Century, 1964.

South Pacific, a Musical Play (music by Richard Rodgers; lyrics by Oscar Hammerstein II; adapted from *Tales of the South Pacific*). New York: Random House, 1949.

The Fires of Spring. New York: Random House, 1949. Bantam Books (paperbound), 1951.

Return to Paradise. New York: Random House, 1951. Bantam Books (paperbound), 1952. Serial publication: "Australia," *Holiday,* VIII (November, 1950), 98-109; "Circles in the Sea," *Holiday,* VII (May, 1950), 68-71; "Fiji," *Holiday,* VII (June, 1950), 60-63; "Guadalcanal," *Holiday,* VIII (August, 1950), 66; "Guadalcanal Today," *Reader's Digest,* LVIII (June, 1951), 105-8; "Mr. Morgan," *Ladies' Home Journal,* LXIII (May, 1951), 58-59; "Myna Birds," *Holiday,* VIII (July, 1950), 26-29; "New Guinea," *Holiday,* VIII (December, 1950), 73; "New Zealand," *Holiday,* IX (January, 1951), 44-47. Collected: "Mr. Morgan," in Bennett Cerf, *Reading for Pleasure,* New York: Harper, 1957.

The Voice of Asia. New York: Random House, 1951. Bantam Books (paperbound), 1952.

The Bridges at Toko-Ri. New York: Random House, 1953. Bantam Books (paperbound), 1955. Originally complete in *Life,* XXXV (July 6, 1953), 58-62.

Sayonara. New York: Random House, 1954. Bantam Books (paperbound), 1955. Originally "Sayonara Means Goodbye," *McCalls,* LXXXI (October, November, December, 1953), 30-31, 30-31, 38-39.

The Floating World. New York: Random House, 1955. Excerpt, "Magic Hand of Hokusai," *Reader's Digest,* LXXIV (June, 1959), 236-38.

The Bridge at Andau. New York: Random House, 1957. Bantam Books (paperbound), 1957. Condensation, *Reader's Digest,* LXX (March, 1957), 23-30; (May, 1957), 93-98.

Rascals in Paradise (with A. Grove Day). New York: Random House, 1957. Bantam Books (paperbound), 1958. Chapter I, abridged, in *This Week* (May 5, 12, 19, 26, 1957); see also June 2, 1957, p. 26. Chapter X, abridged, in *True* (February, 1958), 36-39.

The Hokusai Sketchbooks: Selections from the Manga. Tokyo: Charles E. Tuttle Co., 1958.

Japanese Prints: From the Early Masters to the Modern. Tokyo: Charles E. Tuttle Co., 1959.

Hawaii. New York: Random House, 1959. Bantam Books (paperback), 1961. Excerpt, "Birth of Hawaii," *Life,* XLVII (October 26, 1959), 154-56. Excerpt, "Some Americans from Hawaii," *Reader's Digest,* LXXIV (December, 1959), 82-89.

Report of the County Chairman. New York: Random House, 1961.

Bantam Books (paperback), 1961. Excerpt, "Inside Kennedy's Election," *Look*, XXV (May 9, 1961), 56-60.

The Modern Japanese Print. Tokyo: Charles E. Tuttle Co., 1962.

Caravans. New York: Random House, 1963. Condensed in *Ladies' Home Journal*, LXXX (July-August, 1963), 79-86.

3. *Serial and Miscellaneous Publications*

"Afghanistan: Domain of the Fierce and the Free," *Reader's Digest*, LXVII (November, 1955), 161-72.

"All for One: A Story from Korea," *Reader's Digest*, LXI (July, 1952), 1-2.

"Aloha for the Fiftieth State," New York *Times Magazine*, April 19, 1959, pp. 14-15.

"American in Tahiti," review of autobiography of James Norman Hall, *Paradise of the Pacific*, Honolulu, LXV (January, 1953), 28-29.

"Battle for Burma," *Reader's Digest*, LXXII (April, 1958), 107-13.

"Blunt Truths About Asia," *Life*, XXX (June 4, 1951), 96-100; excerpt in *Reader's Digest*, LIX (September, 1951), 73-78.

"Chances Against the Beginning Writer," in *The Writer's Book*, ed. Helen R. Hull, New York: Harper, 1950, pp. 102-10.

"Chinese Success Story," *Life*, XXXI (December 31, 1951), 76-81.

"The Conscience of the Contemporary Novel," in *The Arts in Renewal*, ed. Sculley Bradley, Philadelphia, University of Pennsylvania Press, 1951, 107-40.

"An Eastern Art Goes Western," *Horizon*, II (May, 1960), 102-14.

"Empty Room," (story), *Ladies' Home Journal*, LXIV (September, 1947), 72-73.

"Facts About the GI Babies," *Reader's Digest*, LXIV (March, 1954), 5-10.

Foreword to Dan Kurzman, *Kishi and Japan: The Search for the Sun*, New York: Obolensky, 1960.

Foreword to José Rizal, *The Lost Eden* (translation by León María Guerrero of *Noli Me Tangere*), Bloomington: University of Indiana Press, 1961.

"Forgotten Heroes of Korea," *Saturday Evening Post*, CCXXIV (May 10, 1952), 19-21.

"4,100 Miles on a Raft," review of *Kon-Tiki*, by Thor Heyerdahl, *Saturday Review of Literature*, XXXIII (September 23, 1950), 12-13.

"Frances Sabin Gets People to Buy Books They Didn't Know They Wanted," *Publisher's Weekly*, CLXXIX (January 9, 1961), 31-34.

"Gift of Phan Tat Thanh," *Reader's Digest*, LXIX (September, 1956), 163-64.

"Happy Talk: Tribute to the Writers of 'South Pacific'," New York *Times*, July 3, 1949, II, 1.

"Hardest-Working Women in the World," *Reader's Digest*, LXXIV (March, 1959), 42-46.

"Hawaii," *Holiday*, XIII (May, 1953), 34-35; excerpts in *Reader's Digest*, LXIII (August, 1953), 102-7.

"Hawaii: The Case for Our Fiftieth State," *Reader's Digest*, LXXIII (December, 1958), 158-60.

"Hawaii the Fiftieth State," New York *Times Magazine*, April 19, 1961, VI, p. 14; also editorial note, May 10, 1961, VI, p. 4.

"Hawaii Politics," series of five articles in Honolulu *Star-Bulletin*, 1958: "Governor Quinn's Great Start," November 1, II, 2; "Ben Dillingham Called Hero of Election," November 8, II, 2; "How to Lose an Election," November 15, II, 2; " 'Four Smart Girls' of the First State Election," November 22, II, 2; " 'How Things Now Look' to Michener," November 21, II, 2.

Hawaiian Airlines, Ltd. A special report to the stockholders. Testimony of J. A. Michener, October 28, 1959.

"Hawaiian Holidays," *Look*, XXIV (December 20, 1960), 31-32.

"Hawaii's Statehood Urged," New York *Times*, January 1, 1959, p. 30; letter dated from Honolulu, December 14, 1958.

"Historic Meeting in Indonesia," *Reader's Digest*, LXVII (August, 1955), 75-79.

"I Would Not Minimize That Apprenticeship," tape-recorded interview before writing classes of Sylvan Karchmer and Ralph J. Salisbury at University of Oregon, *Northwest Review*, IV (Spring, 1961), 5-27. Excerpts, "Thoughts on Writing," *Writer*, LXXV (May, 1962), 12-13; "Two-Finger Exercise," *Beacon*, Honolulu, I (May, 1961), 8-9.

"Indonesia, Islands of Beauty and Turmoil," *Reader's Digest*, LXVII (September, 1955), 30-38.

"International Maturity: A Report on Asia," *Vital Speeches*, XXII (December 15, 1955), 147-51 (speech as president of Fund for Asia, Inc., New York, October 5, 1955).

Introduction to Keyes Beech, *Tokyo and Points East*. New York: Doubleday, 1954.

Introduction to W. W. Davenport, *et al, Hawaii, 1961,* Fodor's Modern Guides, New York: David McKay, 1961, pp. 5-8.

Introduction to A. Grove Day and Carl Stroven (eds.), *A Hawaiian Reader,* New York: Appleton-Century-Crofts, 1959, pp. xi-xvii.

Introduction to Bob Krauss, *Here's Hawaii,* New York: Coward-McCann, 1960, pp. 7-9.

Introduction to Oliver Statler, *Modern Japanese Prints,* Tokyo: Charles E. Tuttle Co., 1956, xv-xvii.

Introduction to Carl Stroven and A. Grove Day (eds.), *The Spell of the Pacific,* New York: Macmillan, 1949, pp. vii-xi.

"Islàm: The Misunderstood Religion," *Reader's Digest,* LXVI (May, 1955), 67-75.

"Japan," *Holiday,* XII (August, 1952), 26-41.

"Kabuki is a Must for America," *Theater Arts,* XXXVIII (March, 1954), 74-75.

"Legacy: The Australian Way," *Reader's Digest,* LXVIII (March, 1956), 57-60.

Letter to Clarice B. Taylor, Honolulu *Star-Bulletin,* July 28, 1961, p. 18, concerning reception in Honolulu of New York interview of previous April.

"Madame Butterfly in Bobby Sox," *Reader's Digest,* LXIX (October, 1956), 21-27.

"Magic Malaya," *Reader's Digest,* LXXIII (September, 1958), 228-40.

"Main Line," *Holiday,* VII (April, 1950), 34-37; abridged in B. A. Botkin, *Sidewalks of America,* Indianapolis: Bobbs-Merrill, 1954.

"Mexico's Mild-Mannered Matador," *Reader's Digest,* LXXIX (July, 1961), 202-4.

"My Other Books," *Harper's Magazine,* CCXXII (January, 1961), 42-44.

"Mystery of Angkor," *Holiday,* XII (November, 1952), 44-47.

"Of Men and Ships: Favorite Tales of the Sea," *Life,* LIII (December 21, 1962), 96-98.

"One Must Respect Korean Culture," *Reader's Digest,* LXIV (April, 1954), 15-19.

"Out to Pasture," see "Empty Room" above (story), *Nation's Business,* XXXVII (April, 1949), 32-33.

"Pakistan: Divided It Stands," *Reader's Digest,* LXV (November, 1954), 136-46.

"People of the Pacific," *Saturday Review,* XLIII (November 12, 1960), 41-43.

"Perfect Teacher," *Coronet*, XXX (June, 1951), 21-24.

"Portraits for the Future," *Saturday Review of Literature*, XXXIV (August 4, 1951), 19-21.

Postscript to Arthur Goodfriend, *Something is Missing*, New York: Farrar, Straus & Young, 1950.

"Present for Aunt Bessie," *Vogue*, CXXXI (March 15, 1958), 107.

"Pursuit of Happiness by a GI and a Japanese," *Life*, XXXVIII (February 21, 1955), 124-26.

"Report from the Frenzied Fifties," New York *Times Magazine*, August 13, 1961, 15.

Review of Andrew Lind, *Race Relations in World Perspective*, Honolulu *Star-Bulletin*, June 12, 1B, 1956 (with Mari Michener).

"Riddle of Pandit Nehru," *Reader's Digest*, LXIX (July, 1956), 96-102.

"Sea of the Talented Travelers," *Saturday Review*, XXXVII (October 23, 1954), 47-48.

"Should Artists Boycott New York?", *Saturday Review*, XLIV (August 26, 1961), 12.

"Some Practical Applications," in Horace M. Lippincott, *Through a Quaker Archway*, New York: Yoseloff, 1959.

"South Pacific," *Saturday Review*, XLII (October 17, 1959), 41.

" 'South Pacific' vs. 'My Fair Lady,' " New York *Times*, XXX, September 23, 1956, II, 1.

"Statehood is Concrete Answer to Reds," Honolulu *Advertiser*, Statehood ed. sec. 12-A, p. 8, June 23, 1959.

"Thailand, Jewel of Asia," *Reader's Digest*, LXV (December, 1954), 57-66.

"This Great Big Wonderful World," *Holiday*, XIX (March, 1956), 40-51.

"This I Believe," *Reader's Digest*, LXV (July, 1954), 143-44. Collected in *This I Believe*, ed. E. R. Murrow, New York: Simon & Schuster, 1954, p. 96-97.

"Today's Wild West: The Great Australian North," *Reader's Digest*, LXVIII (April, 1956), 63-70.

"Tough Man for a Tough Job," *Life*, XXXII (May 12, 1952), 103-6. Condensed in *Reader's Digest*, LXI (August, 1952), 13-16.

"Way It Is in Korea," *Reader's Digest*, LXII (January, 1953), 15-20.

"What Every New Candidate Should Know," New York *Times*, September 23, 1962, VI, 23; reprinted *Reader's Digest*, "Confessions of a Political Candidate," LXXXI (November, 1962), 199-204.

"What Hawaii Means to Me," Honolulu *Star-Bulletin*, July 10, 1954, Saturday section, p. 5.

"When Does Education Stop?" *Reader's Digest*, LXXXI (December, 1963), 153-56.

"While Others Sleep," *Reader's Digest*, LXXI (October, 1957), 68-75.

"Why I Am Running for Congress," *Saturday Evening Post*, CCXXXV (May 5, 1962), 8.

"Why I Like Japan," *Reader's Digest*, LXIX (August, 1956), 182-86.

"Writer's Wars," *Saturday Review*, XXXVIII (January 22, 1955), 44.

"Writing a Book in Hawaii," *Paradise of the Pacific*, Honolulu, LXXI (November, 1959), 154-56.

"Yancy and the Blue Fish" (story), *Ladies' Home Journal*, LXVI (November, 1947), 48-49.

4. Articles on Education

"Bach and Sugar Beets," *Music Educators Journal*, XXV (September, 1938), 29.

"The Beginning Teacher," National Council for the Social Studies, *In-Service Growth of Social Studies Teachers*, 10th Yearbook, 1939, pp. 1-37.

"Discussion in the Schools," *Social Education*, IV (January, 1940), 4-5.

"Functional Social Studies Program," *Curriculum Journal*, IX (April, 1938), 163-64.

(ed.) *Future of the Social Studies*, National Council for the Social Studies, Cambridge, Massachusetts, 1939.

"Idealism Today," *High Points*, XXXI (May, 1949) 13-21; condensed, *Education Digest*, XV (December, 1949), 44-47. Reprinted in E. R. Davis and W. C. Hummel (eds.), *Reading for Opinion*, New York: Prentice-Hall, 2nd ed. 1960, pp. 252-59.

"Improved Unit Method," *Harvard Education Review*, X (March, 1940), 211-24.

"Music and the Social Studies," *Social Studies*, XXVIII (January, 1937), 28-30.

"Participation in Community Surveys as Social Education," in National Council for the Social Studies, *Utilization of Community Resources in the Social Studies*, 9th Yearbook, 1938, pp. 144-63.

"P.E.A. Report," *Social Education,* IV (Deecmber, 1940), 530-31.

"Sex Education: a Success in Our Social-Studies Classes," *Clearing House,* XII (April, 1938), 461-65.

"Steps in Unit Learning and Teaching," Eastern Commercial Teachers' Association, 15th Yearbook, 1942, pp. 58-68.

"Teachers in the Community," *Social Studies,* XXXII (May, 1941), 219-21. Summary in *Progressive Education,* XVII (December, 1940), 546-47.

Unit in the Social Studies; with an introduction by H. E. Wilson. Harvard Workshop Series No. 1. Cambridge, Massachusetts: Harvard University Graduate School of Education, 1940 (with H. M. Long).

"What Are We Fighting For?" *Progressive Education,* XVIII (November, 1941), 342-48.

"Who Is Virgil T. Fry?" *Clearing House,* XVI (October, 1941), 67-70; condensed, *Education Digest,* VII (November, 1941), 4-6; reprinted *Clearing House,* XIX (October, 1944), 69-72; reprinted: *Clearing House* XXIII (September, 1948), 12-16; *Education Digest,* XX (May, 1955), 32-34; *Scholastic,* LXVII (September 22, 1955), 97; condensed, *NEA Journal,* L (September, 1961), 23-24.

5. *Unpublished Materials*

Conversations by A. Grove Day with James A. Michener.
Private correspondence, A. Grove Day and James A. Michener.
Note: For the purpose of collecting data on the activities of a leading author of today, the Library of Congress is amassing the unedited papers of Mr. Michener over a long period. These will be preserved but are not generally accessible.

SECONDARY SOURCES

"Again the Warm Voice of Asia," *Newsweek,* XLIII (January 25, 1954), 92-95, and condensed as "Michener of the South Pacific" in *Reader's Digest,* LXIV (April, 1954), 20. Mainly a review of *The Bridges at Toko-Ri.*

"Artists and Writers," *Newsweek,* LIX (May 14, 1962), 102. Quotes Michener on the pleasures of collecting Japanese prints and modern American painters.

"Author Enacts Own Plot," *Life,* XXXIX (November 7, 1955), 55. A brief, well-illustrated account of Michener's third wedding.

"Author Explains: Why Michener Wrote *The Bridge at Andau*," *Newsweek*, XLIX (March 4, 1957), 104-5. Contains useful information on his activities while covering the Hungarian revolution.

BARRETT, M. E. and M. "On Our List," *Good Housekeeping*, CXLIV (April, 1957), 275-77. Has some personal news and a photograph of the Micheners.

"Biographical Note," New York *Herald-Tribune Book Review* (October 7, 1951), p. 6. Useful information previous to the publication of *The Voice of Asia*.

"Biographical Note," *Saturday Review of Literature*, XXXIV (April 28, 1951), 10. Covers life up to publication of *Return to Paradise*.

BREIT, HARVEY. "Talk with Mr. Michener," New York *Times*, May 22, 1949, VII, 26. Mentions *South Pacific* and the author's ideas on the novelist's function in society.

CLURMAN, ROBERT. "Talk with Mr. Michener," New York *Times Book Review*, March 3, 1957, VII, 18. Deals with experiences in collecting material for *The Bridge at Andau*.

Current Biography, New York: H. W. Wilson Co., 1948, 448-50. An early source of information derived from Michener himself.

HAVIGHURST, W. "Michener of the South Pacific," *English Journal*, XLI (October, 1952), 397-402 and also in *College English*, XIV (October, 1952), 1-6. The only previous appreciation of Michener's novels published by an English professor; gives useful judgments on the early books.

HUTCHINS, J. K. "Man Behind *The Bridges*," New York *Herald-Tribune Books*, July 19, 1953, p. 2. Deals mainly with the preparation of Michener's Korean War novel.

"On an Author," New York *Herald-Tribune Books*, May 20, 1951, p. 3. Deals with the writing of *Return to Paradise*.

INOUYE, HON. DANIEL K. "James A. Michener," speech in House of Representatives by Congressman from Hawaii, September 17, 1962, *Congressional Record*, Proceedings and Debates of the 87th Congress, Second Session. Pays high tribute to Michener as an author, a representative of America in Asia, and a candidate for the House of Representatives.

"James A. Michener Collection of Japanese Prints at the Hawaiian Academy of Arts," *Paradise of the Pacific*, Honolulu, LXXII (November, 1960), 66-67. A brief description with photographs.

KRAUSS, BOB. "Success Story of a Story," *Paradise of the Pacific*, Honolulu, LXXI (November, 1959), 157 (reprinted from column in Honolulu *Advertiser,* September 12, 1959). Reports an interview concerning *Hawaii* just previous to the publication of that novel.

KUNITZ, STANLEY J. *Twentieth Century Authors: First Supplement.* New York: H. W. Wilson Co., 1955, pp. 665-66. Furnished the best biographical information to that date.

LINDLEY, MARION WONG. "Reactions to Michener's *Hawaii,*" *Social Process in Hawaii,* XXIV (1960), 41, 75, 83, 101. Collects a few comments of local readers on the novel.

NATHAN, G. J. "*South Pacific* and Its Criticism," *The Magic Mirror,* New York: Knopf, pp. 250-57. Is less concerned with analyzing the musical comedy than with blasting other schools of Broadway reviewers, but he does call *South Pacific* an "infinitely more intellectual musical than most."

NICHOLS, L. "Talk with Mr. Michener," New York *Times Book Review,* July 12, 1953, p. 16. A discussion of the writing of *The Bridges at Toko-Ri.*

"People Are Talking About . . ." *Vogue,* CXXIX (April 15, 1957), 85. Contains a good portrait of the Micheners not long after publication of *The Bridge at Andau.*

"Personal Glimpses," *Reader's Digest,* LXXXII (January, 1963), 134-35. Gives a brief version of the anecdote concerning Michener's masquerade that enabled him to view the Barnes Collection.

PRESCOTT, ORVILLE. "Novelists and War," *In My Opinion,* Indianapolis: Bobbs-Merrill, 1952, pp. 146-64. Attempts to place Michener in the group of World War II authors; Prescott was one of the first to acclaim *Tales of the South Pacific.*

"Pulitzer Boy," New York *Times,* May 16, 1948, VII, 8. A brief early biography.

SHADDINGER, ANNA E. *The Micheners in America.* Tokyo: Charles E. Tuttle Co., 1958. A prime source for data on Michener's parentage.

SUTTON, HORACE. "The Strange Case of James Michener," *Paradise of the Pacific,* Honolulu, LXXV (September-October, 1963), 21-22. Gives special attention to Michener's relations with Hawaii and contains some biographical information supplied by A. Grove Day.

TAYLOR, CLARICE B., "Michener and Names," *Paradise of the Pacific,* LXXI, Honolulu (October, 1959), 54-55. Mentions the search for names of some of the characters in *Hawaii.*

Selected Bibliography

—————. "More on Michener's *Hawaii*," Honolulu *Star-Bulletin*, June 5, 1960, Women's Section, p. 8. Written by the author's research assistant on his giant novel, notes that her predictions made the previous year have been realized (see below).

—————. "A Preface to a Novel," Honolulu *Star-Bulletin*, Hawaiian Life supplement, June 6, 1959, pp. 2-3. A valuable account of Mrs. Taylor's conversations with Michener and predicts that the novel will arouse much comment in Honolulu.

WARFEL, HARRY R. *American Novelists of Today*. New York: American Book Co., 1951, pp. 299-300. A standard account, now somewhat dated.

WHITBREAD, J., "Private Life of James (*Hawaii*) Michener," *Good Housekeeping*, CL (February, 1960), 28. A brief interview with Michener at his home in Bucks County.

Index